LEGAL KIDNAPPING

From Christopher Columbus to CPS, HOW RICH WHITE MEN HAVE KEPT HUMAN TRAFFICKING ALIVE.

By

David W. Shore

Table of Contents

About The Author

David Shore has been fighting Child Protection Services since December of 2007. My initial reason was to tell my side of the story, and to inform the public of what CPS does to families. As I continued my research, I discovered a connection with Human trafficking, and as I continued to dig deeper, I realized that this has been going on throughout history. That the wealthy always prey upon the less fortunate. The name has changed, as well as the way they have gone to "recruit" new commodities.

Chapter 1

"For a crime to exist, there must be an injured party. There can be no sanction or penalty imposed upon one because of this exercise of Constitutional rights." — Sherar v. Cullen, 481 F. 945

"Our opponents will call us traitors, as if we support another government. In fact, we have pledged our allegiance to something older and wiser than anything that any nation state has to offer, and it is the apologists for the current order who have turned their backs and lost their way." Designed to kill, CrimethInc.com

"Answer the question of who benefits or profits most directly from and action, event, or outcome and you always have the starting point for your analysis or investigation, and sometimes it will also give you the end point." — Sir Arthur Conan Doyle

Human Trafficking! The very words are sickening! It has been around ever since man found out he could make money off his fellow man and woman, and yes! Even children.

As far back as the Egyptians, when they enslaved the Israelites, man has found a way to profit from his fellow human beings; we think of slavery and Human Trafficking as only a black race subject. The truth, as you shall see, goes far beyond that, and it begins with the first white slave trader. You know who he is, but let's introduce him anyway.

In 1492, Cristoforo Columbo (also known as Christopher Columbus) said in his journal, dated October 12, 1492, "No sooner had we concluded the formalities of taking possession of the island than people began to come to the beach..; they are friendly and well-dispositioned people who bear no arms except for small spears.

"They ought to make good and skilled servants.., I think they can easily be made

Christians, for they seem to have no religion. If it pleases Our Lord, I will take six of them to Your Highnesses when I depart." (from Colombo's log, October 12, 1492)

This was from the 1992 article, "500 YEARS OF INDIGENOUS RESISTANCE." (OHTOH-KIN newspaper)

In that article, as I will show here, as well as other areas, the movement of Human

Trafficking has changed labels. It still continues but under a different name: CHILD PROTECTIVE SERVICES. Even the "Product" has changed names: Children instead of families.

Payment is still made but under the name "Bonus" from the Adoption and Safe Families Act of 1997 (then-President Bill Clinton, who gave all the credit to his wife, Hillary Clinton, signed the bill into law).

BEFORE the rich white man arrived in the New World (notice how it is said), the INDIGENOUS people (native Indians) lived peacefully amongst themselves.

They were farmers, fishermen, and hunters.

There were no borders, walls, or even state lines.

No prisons! No homeless!

No courts! Each tribe dealt with rule breakers in the tribe itself. Never was the perpetrator sent away unless it was under banishment. Then, it had to be severe.

The tribe and tribal council consisted of men who discussed each matter, and the decision was final. No appeals!

Their world went without challenge until the arrival of Christopher Columbus in 1492. That's when things changed, not just for the indigenous people but the world as a whole.

This entry in Christopher Columbus' journal should show this and future rich white men's thoughts on everyone else:

"...Your Highnesses must resolve to make them [the Taino-Oh-Toh_kin ed] Christians. I believe that if this effort commences, in a short time, a multitude of people will be converted to our Holy Faith, and Spain will acquire great domains and riches and all of their villages. Beyond doubt, there is a very great amount of gold in this country...

Also, there are precious stones and pearls and an infinite quantity of spices."

Further, Christopher Columbus wrote in his log, "...those people are very unskilled in arms. Your Highnesses will see this for yourselves when I bring you the seven that I have taken. After they learn our language, I shall return them unless your Highness orders that the entire population be taken to Castille or held captive here. With 50 men you could subject everyone and make them do what you wished."

From the very beginning, those who were NOT rich, white males were considered as "property" to be bought and sold. They were no longer and no less a "commodity" to be used as the "owner" deemed.

Slavery was abolished, but there are still those in power, those who have money, who still believe that EVERY PERSON HAS HIS OR HER PRICE! That each person is for sale! Many business owners, including the President, believe that employees are no more and no less than something that can be bought and sold at will. That the employee is either an asset, a liability, or a debt. One that needs to be let go. Why else do companies lay off their best workers, all in the name of profit?

INDIGENOUS "Property" (slaves) eventually were replaced with African "Property" (slaves). The result was the same.

The rich white man "taxed" first the INDIGENOUS, then the African slaves. This gave them more money and control over their "Property" or "Commodity". It is insulting to call INDIGENOUS

Indians and Black persons "Property" and "Commodities", but this is what they were (as I have said, some rich white men, and not-so-rich white men, still consider Indians and Blacks in this manner. Not right at all).

After the Emancipation Proclamation was made and The Thirteenth **Amendment**

(**Amendment** XIII) to the United States Constitution was passed, many believed slavery, and more importantly, the buying and selling of persons was abolished, but the rich white man had other ideas.

In Child Protective Services: HISTORICAL OVERVIEW, CURRENT SYSTEM, by William Wesley Patton and CURRENT SYSTEM.

William Wesley Patton, the author, speaks of the history of CPS, as well as the current system, at the time of the article. William Wesley Patton states, "No ancient civilization considered child protection to be a governmental function. In ancient Rome, for instance, fathers were vested with an almost unlimited natural right to determine the welfare of their children. The welfare of minors was a family matter, not a governmental interest or obligation. Most other governments of the ancient world provided no limits to a father's right to inflict corporal punishment, including infanticide."

In English Common Law, the law was very clear. Read and understand why we have not changed and how kidnapping and slavery still exist today.

In addition to the case-by-case determinations by the chancery court regarding children's property and guardianships, Parliament, in 1601, promulgated the Poor Law Act, which, among other provisions, provided the government jurisdiction to separate children from pauper parents and to place poor children in apprenticeships until the age of majority (21 for males and 16 for females). In 1660, Parliament passed the Tenures Abolition Act, which presaged the end of feudalism, including guardianships in chivalry that had formed the basis for the earlier Court of Wards and Court of Chancery over the guardianship of both children's and the Crown's inheritance and property interests. ("Guardianships in chivalry" provided that when a tenant on a lord's land died, leaving an heir under the age of majority, the lord could control the minor heir's inheritance until the child became an adult.) The Tenures Abolition Act was revolutionary because it vested in the father the right to appoint a guardian for his child heir, which was previously forbidden under the feudal inheritance laws."

Things began to change for fathers in 1660. Let's see how much it changed: "From 1660 until 1873, the Court of Chancery administered equity jurisdiction in conflicts between private parties over testamentary guardianships. It was during these equity determinations that the Court of Chancery expanded the substantive scope of child protection to include, in addition to inheritance and property, concerns over a ward's rights to marry, to a particular type of education or school, to the choice of religious training, and to child custody arrangements. In 1839 Parliament dramatically expanded the court's jurisdiction to determine the best interest of children through the Custody of Infants Act, which provided court jurisdiction to override a father's parental rights, including rights to custody and visitation. Most historians would agree that by the nineteenth century, governmental concern in the child's best interest was perfected directly through the doctrine of *parens patriae,* rather than indirectly through legal contests over property and override a father's parental rights, including the rights to custody and visitation." Sound familiar? Another part reads, "Most historians would agree that by the nineteenth-century, governmental concern in the child's best interest were perfected directly through the doctrine of *parens patriae,* rather than indirectly through legal contests over property and guardianships."

Maybe when our founding fathers came to this country, things changed. Let's find out. "The American Colonies" "The child protection policies of the early American colonists closely mirrored those of seventeenth-and eighteenth-century Britain. The colonists emphasized two aspects of English child protection theory: "the common law rules of family government; and the traditions and child-care practices of the Elizabethan Poor Laws of 1601" (Thomas, p. 299).

Although colonial remedies of placing pauper children into involuntary apprenticeships or into poorhouses initially followed English legal customs, colonial theorists soon expanded court jurisdiction over juveniles to include contexts beyond poverty.

For instance, in eighteenth-century Virginia, courts separated children not just from poor parents but also from parents who were not providing "'good breeding,' neglecting their formal education, not teaching a trade, or were idle, dissolute, unchristian or 'incapable'" (Rendleman, p. 210). Calvinist notions of poverty as idleness and sin permitted court expansion into the normative definitions of the "best interest" of children." So, it appears that rich white men were dictating where your children were to be raised, NOT YOU! Just like Christopher Columbus and the INDIGENOUS people, and then later the AFRICAN people. Am I wrong? Let's see what happened in the 1800's.

"Until the mid1800s, child protection laws did not differentiate among different classes of children; so that dependent children, status offenders, and juvenile delinquents were either housed together in poorhouses with adults or involuntarily apprenticed. However, by 1830, "an embryonic reform movement had begun," which removed dependent children from the teeming poorhouses and placed them in large orphan asylums. (Thomas, pp. 302–303). Due to the refugee movement (1824–1857), private corporations such as the New York House of Refuge (founded in 1824) received public funds and cared for both neglected and delinquent children in large institutions that separated juveniles from adult criminals and paupers. However, by the mid-1850s, an anti-institution movement had developed, with the goal of placing poor city children in country foster placements rather than in large city institutions. Even though numerous state statutes were promulgated in the nineteenth century to care for abused and neglected children, government machinery was inadequate to implement sufficient protection."

Seems children would have been better off with their biological families than with what was in place at that time. This cannot be how things continue. Surely, the government had a better plan. "In 1875 in New York, the first Society for the Prevention of Cruelty to Children (SPCC) was founded to help enforce child protection laws. However, since the SPCC was composed primarily of "wealthy, white men, almost all of them Protestant," who hired middle-class men as family investigators, the families that were targeted were largely poor immigrant families who were judged by middle-class mores and vague standards such as "without proper parental guardianship" (Schiff, p. 413).

The numerous competing reform movements and children's aid societies of the mid-to-late 1800s focused on the child as a member of a family group, not as an autonomous individual, and most emphasized removing children from their own families and placing them into a different home environment. By 1879, the New York

Children's Aid Society had sent 48,000 children out of New York to live with other families. After its first fourteen years, the New York Society for the Prevention of Cruelty to Children "investigated nearly 70,000 complaints of ill-treatment of 209,000 children. Prosecutions were pursued in 24,500 of these cases, resulting in almost 24,000 convictions and the removal of 36,300 children."

WHAT? Things got WORSE for children and for their biological parents! DID I READ CORRECTLY? Let's see one part again. "The SPCC was composed primarily of "wealthy, white men, almost all of them Protestant," who hired middle-class men as family investigators. The families that were targeted were largely poor immigrant families, who were judged by middle-class mores and vague standards such as "without proper parental guardianship." So, just as today, investigators, middle-class men, targeted poor families who were judged by middle-class mores and vague standards.

Are you seeing a pattern here? Let's continue. "By the beginning of the twentieth century, the tide had turned away from family separation and toward family preservation. At the 1909 White House Conference on the Care of Dependent Children, it was declared that "home life is the highest and finest product of civilization. It is the great molding force of mind and of character" (Tanenhaus, p. 550). The twentieth century ushered in a dramatic shift away from private child protective services in favor of governmental control by public agencies authorized under both federal and state child protection statutory schemes.

In 1899, Illinois promulgated the first juvenile court, whose stated purpose was to provide for the care and custody of children in a manner that was an alternative to that of their parents. By 1920, all but three states had a juvenile court system." YEAH!!! Finally, it appeared things were looking up. The family would NOT be separated. But wait! "But the goal of family reunification was rarely realized by the early juvenile courts because few services were made available to assist poor, uneducated parents in curing the conditions that led to state intervention. Instead, children remained in out-of-home placements for considerable periods of time.

For instance, in Chicago, the city with the nation's first juvenile court, the rate of family reunification in 1921 was about the same as in 1912 (70%), but in 1921, more children were staying in institutions for longer periods than in 1912." So, the laws changed, but the result didn't. Maybe we should check the Constitution to see if things can be made better.

"The Constitution and Child Protection Laws," between 1875 and 1900, had numerous challenges to the vague legal definitions of child dependency, and the informal legal proceedings to the separation of parents and children were denied. Early court decisions did not speak in terms of parents' constitutional rights to rear their children, did not closely circumscribe the state's *parens patriae* power to protect children, rejected arguments based upon criminal law analogies, and failed to articulate procedural due process protections for families caught in the child protection legal maelstrom."

In short, parents did not have rights to their own children. I always believed that IF you conceived a child and gave birth to that child, the child was YOUR child to raise as you see fit. Maybe I am missing something. Let's continue and find out.

"Although state and county juvenile courts continued to evolve and to provide different levels of due process in child protection proceedings, the modern child dependency court development was shaped by several decisions of the U.S. Supreme Court, which formalized the court process. In *Meyers v. Nebraska* (1923), the Court held that parents have a fundamental constitutional liberty interest in rearing their children.

Based upon that liberty interest, the Court held in *Lassiter v. Department of Social Services* (1981) that, under certain circumstances, parents are entitled to court-appointed attorneys when they face involuntary termination of their parental rights in child protection proceedings. In Santosky v. Kramer (1982), the Court held that the state has the burden of demonstrating, by clear and convincing evidence, that termination of parental rights is necessary to protect children. Local juvenile courts no longer had unbridled discretion to informally and permanently separate parents and children.

However, the U.S. Constitution became the sounding board only in cases involving permanent severance of parental rights. States are still free to provide fewer due-process procedural rights in temporary child protection cases." It seems that the courts have stated we, as parents, "have a fundamental constitutional liberty interest in rearing their children." Unfortunately, States are still free to provide fewer due-process procedural rights in temporary child protection cases. So, where do we go from here? The authors go further to explain this.

Federal Statutory Policy: In the 1980s and 1990s, the autonomy of state child protection schemes was further compromised and homogenized by a series of federal statutes. In 1980, Congress passed the first comprehensive federal child protective services act, the Adoption Assistance and Child Welfare Act of 1980 (Pub. L. 96-272), which focused on state economic incentives to substantially decrease the length and number of foster care placements.

This act also required specific family reunification services, reflecting the goals of the 1909 White House Conference. However, in 1997, in order to cure many of the defects in the 1980 act, Congress passed the Adoption and Safe Families Act, which shifted the focus from family reunification to expeditious permanency for children in adoptive placements. All state child protection systems adopted the federal guidelines as a requirement for receiving federal subsidies. Thus, because of constitutional and federal statutory requirements, the genesis of America's child protection system has led to great uniformity among state programs." It appears we still have a very long way to go. The goal was reunification, NOT permanency in foster homes or adoption.

So, let's recap:

1. Christopher Columbus kidnaps and sells INDIGENOUS people, thus making them slaves.

2. When the INDIGENOUS people began to dwindle due to dying in mines and overwork, the Spaniards decided to go to Africa, kidnap and purchase the people there, and sell them back home and in countries such as Great Britain and a new country called the United States.

3. Slavery was abolished on January 31, 1865. So, a new "commodity" had to be found. That "commodity" was none other than our own children. The government said to poor and immigrant families that it was in "the best interest of children" that the children be removed, NOT FOR ABUSE OR NEGLECT, BUT FOR POVERTY!

Want MORE proof this is still going on? Read further and decide for yourself.

How about the crisis on the Mexican/United States border? Think that it began under President Trump? How about the militarization of the border? Separation of families? What if I were to tell you that this actually started under another administration, and the current administration continues it? In 1994, the Clinton Administration launched Operation Gatekeeper, a program that massively increased funding for Border Patrol operations in the San Diego sector of the border in California. The federal government greatly enforced this sector and built a fourteen-mile wall between San Diego and Tijuana.

Operation Gatekeeper roughly marks the beginning of a two-decade-running process of ever-increasing border militarization that has continued steadily throughout the Clinton, Bush, and Obama Administrations (and also the Trump Administration). This means that every year, there are more Border Patrol agents, National Guardsmen, helicopters, fences, towers, checkpoints, sensors, guns, and dogs along the border. Understanding the nature of this militarization will go a long way towards clarifying what's actually happening and why." *designed to kill, author unknown*

So, IF this acceleration of Militarization on the border began with President Clinton, to what end? Ever heard of the CCA (Corrections Corporation of America) or the American Legislative Exchange Council (ALEC)? You have not? Not surprising! Many Americans don't. How about Arizona State Bill 1070, which, among other things, would require police to lock up anyone they stop who cannot show proof of having entered the country legally? This was drafted in December of 2009 at the Grand Hyatt hotel in Washington, D.C. So, who deported more in one year? Let's look.

Between 1997 and 2001, during the Presidency of Bill Clinton, about 870,000 people were deported from the United States.

Between 2001 and 2008, during the Presidency of George W. Bush, about 2 million people were deported from the United States.

Between 2009 and 2016, during the Presidency of Barack Obama, about 2.9 million people were deported from the United States.

Under Trump, ICE deportations fell to 226,119 in fiscal 2017, then ticked up to over 250,000 in fiscal 2018 and hit a Trump administration high of 282,242 this fiscal year (as of June).

So, in ONE year, the number of Donald Trump deported in a fiscal year is 282,242.

If we need the illegals for the work most Americans won't do, then why does ICE go and capture them and deport them? The answer is from the unknown author of the essay, "Designed to kill, from CrimethInc.com: "First of all, it's as plain as day that the economy of the United States of America is dependent in no small part on the hyper-exploitation of undocumented labor."

"...if the government were to actually build a two-thousand-mile-long Berlin Wall tonight and then somehow round up and deport every undocumented person in the country tomorrow, there would be massive and immediate disruption in the agriculture and animal exploitation industries, not to mention in everything related to construction- quite possibly leading to a serious breakdown in the national food distribution network and conceivably even famine."

The author also states what I have stated earlier, "Like the rest of the Western Hemisphere, the land that is currently called the United States of America was stolen from its rightful inhabitants by European colonists through a well-documented orgy of bloodshed, massacre, treachery, and genocide of proportions so epic that they are arguably unprecedented in the thousands of other gruesome years of human history preceding them and unsurpassed in the hardily tranquil ones that followed. This monstrous crime has been in progress for over five hundred years, has never been atoned for in any meaningful way, and continues to be perpetrated to this day."

Sounds like rich white men continue to do what they want, without any regard for whom they harm, as long as it is "Business and usual." (why else is the President of the United States a Businessman?)

So, you may be asking, "What does this have anything to do with Human Trafficking or Legal Kidnapping?" In a word, EVERYTHING! Did you, the reader, notice what WASN'T said? How about a WARRANT OR COURT ORDER TO DEPORT? Is ICE above the law, where they DO NOT NEED A WARRANT OR COURT ORDER to arrest and deport illegals?

Sounds like what CPS does, don't you think?

Now, let's see how this applies to the following stories. See if you can see how the government profits from buying and selling people.

If you really want to hear about it, the first thing you'll want to know is how my family's nightmare began.

It all began on December 19, 2007, in South Bend, Indiana. That's the day the nightmare with the Indiana Department of Child Services, or what you know as Child Protective Services, began.

The day began just like all the other days: getting both my son Scott (14 years old at the time and Autistic) and my daughter Emily (age 12 at the time and moderately mentally handicapped) ready for school. Emily was attending Jackson Middle School in South Bend, Indiana, and Scott was attending Riley High School, also in South Bend, Indiana. Scott had graduated from Jackson Middle School a few months earlier. We were all living at 1816 S. William Street in South Bend, Indiana with my wife, Ellen at the time.

Scott was watching his favorite cartoon, Transformers Armada, and Emily was taking her bath with her mother, Ellen, who was assisting her. After 15 minutes, Ellen, behind the closed door of the bathroom, told Emily, "Emily! We need to hurry up so you and your brother can go eat before you two go to school". I asked Scott to get dressed, and he said, "Okay, Dad." During this encounter, I received a strange feeling that I should keep Scott and Emily home. I ignored it. After all, it was just a feeling. Little did I know, I should have kept them home because of what would happen next.

At about 8:45 am, I received a call from Emily's school. I wondered what the school wanted. I answered the phone, but instead of the school principal or one of Emily's teachers on the other end, a St. Joseph County Indiana Department of Child Services Child Protection Services social worker, by the name of Kenneth Downs, was on the other end. When I asked why he was calling me from Emily's school, Mr. Downs stated his office received a call from a teacher at Jackson Middle School that Emily may have been molested by her brother Scott. I asked who had said Scott had molested his sister, and Mr. Downs stated he was not at liberty to discuss the person's name (later, I discovered the teacher was a new teacher, Mrs. Ivory, who did not like Emily).

Mr. Downs stated that the teacher noticed Emily walking down the hallway from the girls' restroom, walking funny. When Mrs. Ivory asked Emily why she was walking funny, Mrs. Ivory stated that Emily had told her that her brother Scott had washed her with a concoction of dog shampoo and regular shampoo.

We had two dogs at the time: a Jack Russell Terrier named Lady and a Jack Russell/ Labrador Retriever named Jack. Mrs. Ivory also stated Emily said Scott was dancing around in the shower with Emily and also kissed her chest, privates, and buttocks. This never happened because, as I stated in the beginning, Emily's mother, Ellen, was in the bathroom with Emily, assisting her with her bath.

Mr. Downs stated he was to interview Emily, and I asked if I should be there, to which Mr. Downs stated I did not have to be there. Mr. Downs then hung up the phone. A few minutes later, another call came in. This time, it was from a South Bend Special Victims Unit Officer named Galen Peletier. The detective stated the exact same thing Mr. Downs said. Both also said they would interview Scott at his school after they finished at Jackson Middle School interviewing Emily. Detective Peletier hung up the phone.

At about 9:30 am, I received a call from Detective Peletier. He said he interviewed both Scott and Emily. He felt something wasn't right. Nothing indicated Scott had done anything, and Emily didn't act like she was afraid of Scott, even though Mr. Downs insisted Emily said she was afraid of her brother. The detective said, with our permission, to place Scott at Madison Center Hospital, in South Bend, Indiana, instead of arresting Scott for molesting his sister.

He wanted to ask his supervisor to see about getting approval. I said okay. About 5 minutes later, the detective called, saying Scott would be going to Madison Center Hospital; against the strong insistence, Scott was arrested. Emily would be returning home. Emily wouldn't be with us for much longer.

On December 21, 2007, at Scott's initial hearing (Scott was never charged yet had a hearing anyway at the Juvenile Justice Center in South Bend, Indiana),

Scott wasn't there. My wife Ellen and I, with Emily, arrived early. Mr. Downs met us and reassured us, saying that CPS doesn't separate families.

The judge on Scott's case was Judge Peter J. Neimeth. When it was our turn, as we began to enter the courtroom, Mr. Downs said Emily wasn't allowed in the courtroom. Mr. Downs volunteered to watch Emily, along with a St. Joseph County deputy Sheriff. Ellen and I told Emily that we would be right back; just had to speak to the judge. During the hearing, I thought I had heard Emily yelling for Ellen and me. When I attempted to leave the courtroom, another St. Joseph County officer blocked the door, preventing me from leaving.

After Ellen and I were done at Scott's hearing, we left but did not see Emily, Mr. Downs, or the deputy sheriff. We were instructed to go to the basement of the juvenile courtroom, where everything would be explained. We headed down to the basement, but as we entered one of the rooms, neither Emily nor Mr. Downs was there. Another case worker was there, Ms. Elizabeth Orina.

Ms. Orina had been assigned to Emily. When I asked why, Ellen and I were informed that Mr. Downs and the deputy sheriff stated Ellen and I were yelling at Emily to recant her story. First, that never happened because there were several other people in the hallway at the time. Second, there was video surveillance to show we never did that. Ellen and I had another court appearance with Judge Neimeth in two days. Ellen and I went home, not realizing our nightmare was just beginning.

At Emily's hearing, Mr. Downs and his supervisor stated:

1. Scott should have been arrested and charged with molesting Emily (to say she was sounding like a mad woman would be an understatement).

2. Ellen and I were yelling at Emily to recant her story. When I attempted to explain that the incident never happened, Judge Neimeth said he didn't want to hear it. The court ordered supervised visitation, to be determined by the Department of Child Services. Ellen and I went home again and felt this Christmas would be one we would never forget.

We never missed a visit, first with Scott at Madison Center. There was always a person there writing down everything we did and said. It wasn't until January that we had our supervised visitation with Emily at the Families First Center in South Bend, Indiana.

Chapter 2

If you really want to hear about it, the first thing you'll want to know is how my family's nightmare began.

It all began on December 19, 2007, in South Bend, Indiana. That's the day the nightmare with the Indiana Department of Child Services, or what you know as Child Protective Services, began.

The day began just like all the other days: getting both my son Scott (14 years old at the time and Autistic) and my daughter Emily (age 12 at the time and moderately mentally handicapped) ready for school. Emily was attending Jackson Middle School in South Bend, Indiana, and Scott was attending Riley High School, also in South Bend, Indiana. Scott had graduated from Jackson Middle School a few months earlier. We were all living at 1816 S. William Street in South Bend, Indiana, with my wife, Ellen, at the time.

Scott was watching his favorite cartoon, Transformers Armada, and Emily was taking her bath, with her mother, Ellen, assisting her. After 15 minutes, Ellen, behind the closed door of the bathroom, told Emily, "Emily! We need to hurry up so you and your brother can go eat before you two go to school". I asked Scott to get dressed, and he said, "Okay, Dad." During this encounter, I received a strange feeling that I should keep Scott and Emily home. I ignored it. After all, it was just a feeling.

Little did I know, I should have kept them home because of what would happen next.

At about 8:45 am, I received a call from Emily's school. I wondered what the school wanted. I answered the phone, but instead of the school principal or one of Emily's teachers on the other end, a St. Joseph County Indiana Department of Child Services Child Protection Services social worker, by the name of Kenneth Downs was on the other end.

When I asked why he was calling me from Emily's school, Mr. Downs stated his office received a call from a teacher at Jackson Middle School that Emily may have been molested by her brother Scott. I asked who had said Scott had molested his sister, and Mr. Downs stated he was not at liberty to discuss the person's name (later, I discovered the teacher was a new teacher, Mrs. Ivory, who did not like Emily).

Mr. Downs stated the teacher noticed Emily walking down the hallway from the girls' restroom, walking funny. When Mrs. Ivory asked Emily why she was walking funny, Mrs. Ivory stated that Emily had told her that her brother Scott had washed her with a concoction of dog shampoo and regular shampoo.

We had two dogs at the time: a Jack Russell Terrier named Lady and a Jack Russell/ Labrador Retriever named Jack. Mrs. Ivory also stated Emily said Scott was dancing around in the shower with Emily and also kissed her chest, privates, and buttocks. This never happened because, as I stated in the beginning, Emily's mother, Ellen, was in the bathroom with Emily, assisting her with her bath.

Mr. Downs stated he was to interview Emily, and I asked if I should be there, to which Mr. Downs stated I did not have to be there. Mr. Downs then hung up the phone. A few minutes later, another call came in. This time from a South Bend Special Victims Unit Officer named Galen Peletier. The detective stated the exact same thing Mr. Downs said. Both also said they would interview Scott at his school after they finished at Jackson Middle School interviewing Emily. Detective Peletier hung up the phone.

At about 9:30 am, I received a call from Detective Peletier. He said he interviewed both Scott and Emily. He felt something wasn't right. Nothing indicated Scott had done anything, and Emily didn't act like she was afraid of Scott, even though Mr. Downs insisted Emily said she was afraid of her brother. The detective said, with our permission, to place Scott at Madison Center Hospital in South Bend, Indiana, instead of arresting Scott for molesting his sister. He wanted to ask his supervisor to see about getting approval. I said okay. About 5 minutes later, the detective called, saying Scott would be going to Madison Center Hospital against the strong insistence; Scott was arrested. Emily would be returning home. Emily wouldn't be with us for much longer.

On December 21, 2007, at Scott's initial hearing (Scott was never charged yet had a hearing anyway at the Juvenile Justice Center in South Bend, Indiana),

Scott wasn't there. My wife Ellen and I, with Emily, arrived early. Mr. Downs met us and reassured us, saying that CPS doesn't separate families.

The judge on Scott's case was Judge Peter J. Neimeth. When it was our turn, as we began to enter the courtroom, Mr. Downs said Emily wasn't allowed in the courtroom. Mr. Downs volunteered to watch Emily, along with a St. Joseph County deputy Sheriff. Ellen and I told Emily that we would be right back; just had to speak to the judge.

During the hearing, I thought I had heard Emily yelling for Ellen and me. When I attempted to leave the courtroom, another St. Joseph County officer blocked the door, preventing me from leaving. During that hearing, I requested a court-appointed lawyer. Judge Neimeth denied my request.

After Ellen and I were done at Scott's hearing, we left but did not see Emily, Mr. Downs, or the deputy sheriff. We were instructed to go to the basement of the juvenile courtroom, where everything would be explained. We headed down to the basement, but as we entered one of the rooms, neither Emily nor Mr. Downs was there.

Another case worker was there, Ms. Elizabeth Orina. Ms. Orina had been assigned to Emily. When I asked why, Ellen and I were informed that Mr. Downs and the deputy sheriff stated Ellen and I were yelling at Emily to recant her story. First, that never happened because there were several other people in the hallway at the time. Second, there was video surveillance to show we never did that. Ellen and I had another court appearance with Judge Neimeth in two days. Ellen and I went home, not realizing our nightmare was just beginning.

At Emily's hearing, Mr. Downs and his supervisor stated:

1. Scott should have been arrested and charged with molesting Emily (to say she was sounding like a mad woman would be an understatement)

2. Ellen and I were yelling at Emily to recant her story. When I attempted to explain that the incident never happened, Judge Neimeth said he didn't want to hear it. The court ordered supervised visitation, which was to be determined by the Department of Child Services. Ellen and I went home again and felt this Christmas would be one we would never forget.

We never missed a visit. The first was with Scott at Madison Center. There was always a person there writing down everything we did and said. It wasn't until January that we had our supervised visitation with Emily at the Families First Center in South Bend, Indiana.

Chapter 3

"Government implies the power of making laws. It is essential to the idea of a law that it be attended with a sanction or, in other words, a penalty or punishment for disobedience. If there are no penalties annexed to disobedience, the resolutions or commands which pretend to be laws will, in fact, amount to nothing more than advice or recommendation. This penalty, whatever it may be, can only be inflicted in two ways: by the agency of the courts and ministers of justice, or by military force."

The Federalist Papers No. 15: Hamilton, July 28, 2008.

Being Transported to the St. Joseph County Jail seemed unreal. I mean, after all, all I had done was assist my moderately mentally handicapped daughter with her bath when she was eight (8) years old. How can that be illegal?

Indiana law even supports this:

Indiana Code Title 16-18-2-28.5

Attendant Care Services

"Attendant Care Services," for purposes of IC 16-27 -1 and IC 16-27-4 means services: (2) Assistance with routine bodily functions, including,

(A) bathing and personal hygiene.

Even the Social Security Administration, in their Program Operations

Manual System (POMS) states: D. Definition Of Attendant Care Services For purposes of this provision, attendant care services are those forms of assistance that help a person with a disability meet his or her essential needs at home or at work, such as bathing, toileting, dressing, cooking, eating, communicating, traveling to and from work, and similar personal needs.

Why, then, with both Indiana and the Social Security Administration saying that I can assist my daughter with bathing, can I then be charged with Child Molestation? Indiana law gives that answer: Indiana Code Title 35.

Criminal Law and Procedure. IC 35-42-4-3 (B), which reads as follows: (b) A person who, with a child under fourteen (14) years of age, performs or submits to any fondling or touching of either the child or the older person, with intent to arouse or satisfy the sexual desires of either, the child or the older person, commits child molesting, a level 4 felony. (Previous to this version, it was a class c felony).

I was booked into the jail on July 28, 2008.

My court-appointed attorney, Arvil R. Howe, didn't meet with me for at least two weeks. He had received disclosure, which was nothing, but I wasn't allowed to look at my daughter's deposition, nor my wife's, or my own.

Each time I would meet with Mr. Howe and show him cases and give his number of character witnesses, Mr. Howe would always say, " We don't need any of that; it's her word vs. your word." During von Dire's jury selection, a friend of Detective Lancaster's was allowed to be on the jury as the foreman. I objected to Mr. Howe on this, saying he may influence the jury, but Mr. Howe didn't listen to me.

My trial began on January 27, 2009, six months after I was arrested. The only people who testified were:

1. Pam Whisman
2. Detective Tim Lancaster
3. My daughter Emily
4. My wife, at the time, Ellen (who testified for both; the prosecution and me)

On January 29, 2009, after 11 hours of jury deliberation, the jury asked this question:

Could the incident have happened other than the two dates on the affidavit? The prosecution, on January 27, 2009, motioned the court to amend the affidavit to read from this version: On or about the 1st of November 2003 to the 1st of November 2004, when E.S. was eight years old.

To this version: Between the 4th of November 2003 to the 4th of November 2004, when E.S was eight years old.

My judge, John M. Marnocha, after checking some previous cases, stated, "After my review of past cases, it is my opinion that it doesn't matter when the incident happened." Mr. Howe objected but was overruled. 30 minutes later, I was convicted and sentenced to 6 years in prison. The Indiana Appellate Court and my judge denied both my appeal and my Post Conviction Relief.

Now that you have seen how I got here, let's go into how CPS is a

Corruption Protective Service, and how corrupt and rouge it really

is.

You have also read how this began; from 1492, when Christopher

Columbus kidnapped and sold INDIGENOUS people to the King and Queen of Spain, to the kidnapping, purchase, and sale of African people, men, women, and children, to today where CPS, modern-day

Christopher Columbus,' remove your children, saying it is in "**the best interest of children.**"

Do you know who else said this? It was Adolf Hitler.

"The state must declare the child to be the most precious treasure of the people. As long as the government is perceived as working for the benefit of the children, the people will happily endure almost any curtailment of liberty and almost any deprivation."

"They seem never to have recollected the danger from legislative usurpations, which, by assembling all power in the same hands, must lead to the same tyranny as is threatened by Executive usurpations."

The Federalist Papers No. 48:

Madison

Let's look at federal legislation, where CPS is allowed, WITHOUT A WARRANT, to remove children from the home.

It is called the Adoption and Safe Families Act (ASFA) and the Child Abuse Prevention and Treatment Act (CAPTA), which reads in part, "federal funds are made available to the states based on the number of children taken into state care, and the length of time they remain in custody."

Don't believe the federal government pays states to take your children? Here is a quote from the West Virginia Secretary of Health and Human Resources head, Mr. Couch:

"The federal government has always paid us only if we pull children from their homes." (Paid to Pull Children from Their Homes," September 25, 2018, parentalrightsfoundation.org)

Even the former Georgia State Senator Nancy Schaefer stated this in a report entitled "The Corrupt Business of Child Protective Services."

In her report, she states that between $6,000 and $10,000 is paid as a bonus to CPS workers who remove children from the home, regardless of whether the allegations made are proven or not. Even Carlos Morales, former CPS investigator repeats this.

On the website HG.org., in an article titled "Sexual abuse: An epidemic in foster care settings," it says, "Approximately 530,000 children in the United States live in foster care at any given time. Some of these children are placed in foster care because they have been sexually abused, abused in other ways, or neglected. Unfortunately, many of these children are again abused in the foster care setting.

A study by Johns Hopkins University found that children who are in foster care are four times more likely to be sexually abused than other children, not in this setting. Additionally, children who are in group homes are 28 times more likely to be abused than children not living in these homes.

Male and female children may be sexually abused. Likewise, very young children to nearly adult children can be abused in these settings."

Legal action against the foster care system is also stated:

Legal Action Against The Foster Care Agency

Foster care agencies are often required to follow strict protocols regarding how they vet foster parents and conduct extensive background checks. However, these procedures may not always be followed, or a foster parent may develop ways to get around them. In some cases, a foster care agency may be held liable for harm that befalls the child, such as if the foster care agency was negligent in the child's placement. However, sometimes foster care agencies are state governmental programs, which may have immunity from such lawsuits. It is important to contact an experienced lawyer to discuss the possibility of pursuing a claim against a negligent foster care agency.

So, what can someone do if his or her child, or children, are taken away and placed in a foster home? The answer is unless you, as the biological parent, speak up, you have no recourse. So, why, then, since this is going on, does the public allow this to happen? In my personal opinion, it is the man who started the whole thing: JOHN WALSH!

Mr. Walsh has convinced America and CPS that ANYONE accused or convicted of a sex offense, especially when CPS is involved, that the person, usually the father or another male family member, is a MONSTER and needs to be constantly monitored because that person is DANGEROUS.

I will agree that there are people who harm children physically, mentally, and sexually. I am not condoning people who molest or abuse children. That's not the objective of this book. The objective of this book is to reveal to you, the reader, as well as to people like John Walsh, the REAL MONSTERS! Those MONSTERS are the ones who say they are here to "protect the children" and even kidnap them, saying it is Exigent Circumstances.

A legal way of saying that biological parents, especially fathers, are MORE of a threat than those the state says are more qualified. Carlos Morales learned, while a CPS investigator, that our children are NOT ours. They belong to the state. Mr. Morales was trained that way. Children are commodities, like milk or bread. Children are how states get their money. The more children the state takes, the more money the state receives.

You may be asking, "If this is true, then what rights do the parents have?" Unfortunately, the answer is none other than what the state says.

Chapter 4

The United Nations Convention on the Rights of the Child was signed on 20 November 1989 and became effective 2 September 1990. 194 countries are parties to this. The United States is one that did not. This Convention has 20 ratifications.

There are two optional protocols, which were adopted on May 25, 2000. The first optional protocol restricts the involvement of children in military conflicts, and the second optional protocol prohibits the sale of children, child prostitution, and child pornography. Both protocols have been ratified by more than 160 states. The United States ratified these two optional protocols. The Second Optional protocol, which identifies the sale of children, I will be focusing on it. I guess CPS forgot about this or just does not care.

Carlos Morales, in his book Legally Kidnapped, says he was trained to ignore parents' First, second, fourth, fifth, sixth, and Fourteenth Amendment rights. That CPS takes children, many times, without a warrant or court order.

Article 19 of the Convention states that State parties must "take all appropriate legislative, administrative, social and educational measures to protect the child from ALL forms of physical or mental violence." I Guess CPS doesn't include violence in foster care.

Why, then, are we, the public, not informed of this? Matthew Wilcox can explain. He is a former CPS worker from Florida. In an article from the Dothan Eagle online newspaper, dated July 28, 2018, Mr. Wilcox says that he did falsify his reports. The reason he did it: TO KEEP HIS JOB! Mr. Wilcox even stated that he knows every state social worker falsified their reports just to keep their jobs.

A Florida Child Protective Services investigator from Florida, Jason Robert Kent, in an online police report from the Pinellas County Sheriff's Office, online, was arrested on November 28, 2017, for ten counts of falsifying interview records.

On his website, Carlos Morales admits to being guilty of kidnapping children from their parents under the color of law.

Former Georgia State Senator Nancy Schaefer, in a report titled "The Corruption of Child Protective Services, stated, "I believe Child Protective Services nationwide has become corrupt and that the entire system is broken beyond repair. I am convinced parents and families should be warned of the dangers."

Further, Ms. Schaefer talks about drug companies making money off of children: "In one county, a private drug testing business was operating within the agency's department that required many, many drug tests from parents and individuals for profit. It has already made over $100,000." "Having worked with probably 300 cases statewide, and now hundreds and hundreds across this nation and in nearly every state, I am convinced there is no responsibility and no accountability in the Child Protective Services system." — Nancy Schaefer, Corruption of Child Protective Services.

Mrs. Schaefer and her husband were murdered on 26 March 2010, a few months after she released her report.

This has been going on for four decades. Families have been torn apart, all for money. Children are nothing more than property to be bought and sold. Many times, the parents of these children CPS takes are working poor. They are not neglectful, abusive, use drugs, or have mental issues. All it takes is someone making a call to CPS, making an allegation of abuse or neglect, and CPS gets to work to remove your children. It is not in the best interest of the child. It is in the best interest of the business of CPS to remove your children.

So, how do you protect your family from being torn apart? To begin, unless CPS has a warrant or court order, you DO NOT HAVE TO LET THEM IN! The police will even tell you that they cannot enter your home without a warrant or unless you allow them in. SO, DO NOT LET THEM IN! Also, call a lawyer IMMEDIATELY!

RECORD EVERYTHING and inform CPS at the door you are recording them. CPS will say you cannot, or they will say they don't want you to record them. Record them anyway. Document everything that is said and done. CPS will write the reports where it will make you and your spouse to be the most abusive and dangerous parents ever.

Fathers, this is for you. IF you are accused of abusing your child, especially sexually, do not say anything to the CPS social worker unless a lawyer is present, and is working for you.

IF CPS does take your children WITHOUT A WARRANT, get all the information about them.

1. The CPS worker's name, number, and location they are working out of.
2. The CPS worker's supervisor's name.
3. ALL police officers' involved names and badge numbers.
4. ALL reports from CPS and the police.
5. Ask for ALL medical, psychological, and psychiatric reports and results from Doctors and Forensic Child Psychologists.
6. The name of the accuser. Under the 14th Amendment of the United States Constitution, you have the RIGHT to know who is accusing you of harming your children. IF CPS says they do not have to give that information, make sure your lawyer is there to hear it or record them saying it.
7. When the Court goes to place your children, make sure to have family with you that are willing to take your children until the matter is settled.

Remember, CPS violates the 1st, 2nd, 4th, 5th, 6th, 8th, and 14th Amendments of the United States Constitution. They play by their own set of rules. Who allows them to do this? 1st, we did, back in the 1980's. Remember John Walsh? He had everyone to believe our children were in danger from predators. Too bad those predators work for CPS. 2nd, our elected officials. CPS pays them to make sure they are immune from being prosecuted. That's not to say they are not; they are given 11th Amendment immunity simply for being a government agency. How do they make sure? CPS agents, Lawyers, and even Judges give money to each other, but it is called a "campaign contribution."

Learn the Constitution, especially the 1st, 2nd, 4th, 5th, 6th, and 14th Amendments. It will save your family.

I want to thank everyone who helped me complete my book. My late mother and father to whom they told me that I could be and do anything I set my mind to. I thank God for giving me the ability and knowledge to tell my story. All my Facebook friends, my friends Kevin Murry and Kurt Gunty, whom I have known since High School. Thank you to Lisa and Christina. You're my inspiration. Thank you to my daughter, Emily. You have grown up to be a fighter and a woman unto your own. Thank you to my brother Chuck and my brother Rex for kicking me in the butt to get me to keep going. Finally, and this may sound strange, thank you to CPS. They motivated me to write this book. Without their corruption and their actions against my family, I would never have written this book. Finally, thank you, the reader. There are other books to read. Thank you for choosing my book. May what I wrote inspire you to take action.

ACTION AGAINST THIS CORRUPTION PROTECTIVE SERVICE!

THIS ROUGE AGENCY!

YOUTUBE VIDEOS ON CHILD PROTECTIVE SERVICES

"CPS CORRUPTION-OUR STORY," *CPS whirlwind- 2011.*

"Public Testimonies Exposing DCFS/CPS Fraud and misconduct", Sheila Allen April 22, 2017.

"CPS Worker scared of being recorded," Hector Valle, May 7, 2018

"Terrorism, threats, and intimidation by Iowa DHS/CPS," Robert Norman March 27, 2014.

"HUMAN TRAFFICKING ALERT!!" Grassroots CPS October 3, 2018. "ABDUCTIONS IN BROAD DAYLIGHT," Grassroots CPS October 3, 2018.

The Remblis Family, November 30, 2016 (Look under The Remblis Family for all videos).

"DHS/CPS TAKING KIDS WITHOUT A COURT ORDER OVER RUMORS," January 26, 2018.

"INDIANA COUPLE ACCUSED OF ABUSING FOSTER CHILDREN" Local 12, Sept. 7, 2018.

"FOSTER PARENTS WHO STARVED CHILD SENTENCED TO 5-10 YEARS IN JAIL", KMTV 3 News Sept. 15, 2017.

"BABY DIES IN FOSTER CARE HOME", ABC 10 News, Sept. 13, 2016. "FOSTER FAMILY SPEAKS OUT AFTER DEATH OF INFANT," ABC 15 Arizona, October 16, 2015.

"DEATH OF BABY IN FOSTER CARE UNDER INVESTIGATION" WLWT, Feb. 25, 2011.

"BABY DIES IN FOSTER CARE," WFLA News Channel 8, November

7, 2017.

"CPS COERCED US TO "AGREE" TO A SAFETY PLAN! NO FULL DISCLOSURE! WE WERE CLUELESS AND PERFECT TARGETS", Grassroots

CPS Corruption Action, October 7, 2018.

I want to thank everyone who helped me complete my book. My late mother and father to whom they told me that I could be and do anything I set my mind to. I thank God for giving me the ability and knowledge to tell my story. All my Facebook friends, my friends Kevin Murry and Kurt Gunty, whom I have known since High School. Thank you to Lisa and Christina. You're my inspiration. Thank you to my daughter Emily. You have grown up to be a fighter and a woman unto your own. Thank you to my brother Chuck and my brother Rex for kicking me in the butt to get me to keep going. Finally, and this may sound strange, thank you to CPS. They gave me the motivation to write this book. Without their corruption, and their actions against my family, I would never have written this book. Finally, thank you, the reader. There are other books to read. Thank you for choosing my book. May what I wrote inspire you to take action.

IF you need legal help, contact: Vincent W. Davis, Law Offices of Vincent W. Davis & Associates, CA CPS, Defense Law Firm, 150 Santa Anita, CA Arcadia, CA, 91006 (888)888-6582.

If you have legal questions, feel free to call us. Vincent W. Davis has a radio show every Saturday at 10am California Time. http://www.fightchildprotectivesevices. It is the Law firm's website.

I'm Guilty of Child Kidnapping for the State

By **Carlos Morales** from Carlos Morales - CPS Whistleblower link Jul 31, 2014

My name is Carlos Morales and I was an investigator for Child Protective Services, and I'm guilty. I'm guilty of what many other American Citizens are guilty of, which is the belief that CPS has the child's best interest in mind when it commits atrocity after atrocity. I'm guilty of working for an organization that has hampered freedom throughout the United States, and has caused millions of parents to live in fear. I'm guilty of working for an agency that has done more to carry out the war on drugs than the war against child abuse. I'm guilty of working for an agency that has kidnapped children, thrown them in to foster homes, and destroyed their lives. I'm guilty of working for CPS. Within CPS, I did not help children, I hurt. I did not protect families, I helped ruin them. I did not work to benefit society, instead I helped imprison it. Child Protective Services is an agency which damages and controls society from within, by allowing the State to take over the lives of children. As family judge Bryan Lindsey put, "There is no system ever devised by mankind that is guaranteed to rip husband and wife or father, mother and child apart so bitterly than our present Family Court System."

The vile actions and justification for Child Protective Services and the State, in general, can be summarized in just one sentence: The inhumanity of humanity knows no bounds when systems are put in place that justify their injustices. When examining the tyranny by those who've worked for the state, when exposing the evils of *institutionalized dogmas,* when grasping the absurdity of social welfare through collective imprisonment, appeasers of authority will assert that those working within the government are *"just doing their job."* No doubt this is true, and a certain part of me believed that while I was a foot soldier for the kidnapping agency called Child Protective Services.

When I began working for the agency, I had the highest of hopes; I believed I was working for the "best interest of the child." Now that term haunts me, for all those who speak for the "best interest of the child" — whether that be the police, politicians, pundits, propagandists, abusive parents, and public school teachers — are the least likely to ask the child what they actually want in their life. This is the coercive paternalistic nature of the State and is at the core of central planners that are innately tyrannical with their progressive tirades that are backed by the threat of guns/force/jail.

Not a day goes by without a pronouncement by those who seek to control through suggestion first and force second that they have discovered what will solve society's complex issues — know this now: any government regulation/law is a testament to the age-old belief that "might make right."

That might, at its core, is rotten but still those who march off to war against others through the belief in a State refuse to see the gun in the room and the blood on the floor. They're all standing in blood while bickering about who's going to get to hold the gun next. While we bicker about topics and externalities that are mere contradictory abstractions that blur the light of reason, a fair bit of individuals go out and simply "do their jobs." They're the cops who arrest and destroy the lives of individuals, whose crimes were without a victim, they are the drone operators who turn bodies into red debris, whose lives were not centered on the destruction of others, and they are the CPS workers who thrust children into abusive foster homes, whose parents were without fault. The blood that the innocent have shed is rendered meaningless by the obedient public which makes excuses for the executioners: "They may have done wrong, but they were simply taking orders." This is the callous apprehension towards moral culpability that hinders progress towards peace, and pushes us further into never-ending war and conflict. Excusing tyranny is the most tyrannical action that can be done, for it gives free reign to the bringers of death to stomp over the lives of innocent individuals. An empathetic understanding of the plight of those who became soldiers, cops, CPS workers, etc., is absolutely important, but empathy can become a weapon when it prevents us from calling a murderer, a murderer, a kidnapper, a kidnapper, and a thief, a thief. While working for child protective services, I was at odds with my morality – for to act morally would be antithetical to the very nature of the agency. The nature of CPS and the nature of the State are innately parasitical, for rather than create, they steal and hinder creativity; rather than progress society forward through open dialogue and non-violent means, they close any dialogue with the most violent means. Instead of empathetic understanding, they provide the world with cages for anyone codified as socially undesirable. Instead of understanding the roots of injustice, they perpetuate injustices while swinging at the branches and ignoring the root of all evil. My previous work in the State is not something that should be forgiven and I will not ask forgiveness of those that I wronged while working for CPS – instead, I attempt with every breath I take to heed a warning to any man, woman, or child that is ever put in a position to have to deal with them. For a time, I was an arm for the state, and now, I seek to be a hand in helping those who are victims of the state. My guilt is never-ending, and the PTSD that I have suffered from working for the agency is nothing compared to the fear and anguish of parents and children who were victims of the agency. To those who are still working for the system, I beg that you leave now before you hurt another innocent person. I beg those reading this that you work to expose the tyranny that is the State. The inhumanity of humanity knows no bounds when systems are put in place which justifies their injustices. The key to the salvation of humanity is by embracing truth, and to do that we cannot justify evil in the name of good social tact, pseudo-empathy, irrational intellectualism, and a fear of ostracism. The truth is that I was not working in the best interest of the child while working for Child Protective Services; I was working in the best interest of the State, and I was working in the best interest of tyranny. It was in their interest to ruin the lives of others through the manipulation and kidnapping of children for profit – they turned children into products that they would sell for cash. Their existence and my actions were justified continuously by every man and woman who stated that the State knew what was in the best interest of the child. The blood is on their hands, and the blood is on my hands. We can never wash it away, but we can help heal wounds and stop it at the core when we no longer justify the necessity of evil. That evil is the belief that violence can be used to help solve social issues – that evil is the belief in a state. (from www.liberty.org)

This is the report of former Georgia State Senator Nancy Schaefer, concerning CPS. This is from November 16, 2007. Nancy Schaefer and her husband were murdered on March 26, 2010.

From the legislative desk of Senator Nancy Schaefer, 50th District of Georgia, November 16, 2007. THE CORRUPT

BUSINESS OF CHILD PROTECTIVE Services BY: Nancy Schaefer Senator,

SO''''' District

My introduction to child protective service cases was due to a grandmother in an adjoining state who called me with her tragic story. Her two granddaughters had been taken from her daughter who lived in my district. Her daughter was told wrongly that if she wanted to see her children again, she should sign a paper and give up her children. Frightened and young, the daughter did. I have since discovered that parents are often threatened with the cooperation of permanent separation of their children.

The children were taken to another county and placed in foster care. The foster parents were told wrongly that they could adopt the children. The grandmother then jumped through every hoop known to man in order to get her granddaughters. When the case finally came to court, it was made evident by one of the foster parent's children that the foster parents had, at any given time, 18 foster children and that the foster mother had an inappropriate relationship with the caseworker.

In the courtroom, the juvenile judge acted as though she was shocked and said the two girls would be removed quickly. They were not removed. Finally, after much pressure was applied to the Department of Family and Children Services of Georgia (DFCS), the children were driven to South Georgia to meet their grandmother, who gladly drove to meet them. After being with their grandmother two or three days, the judge, quite out of the blue, wrote up a new order to send the girls to their father, who previously had no interest in the case and lived on the West Coast. The father was in "adult entertainment".

His girlfriend worked as an "escort" and his brother, who also worked in the business, had a sexual charge brought against him.

Within a couple of days, the father was knocking on the grandmother's door and took the girls kicking and screaming to California. The father developed an unusual relationship with the former foster parents and soon moved back to the southeast, and the foster parents began driving to the father's residence and picking up the little girls for visits. The oldest child had told her mother and grandmother on two different occasions that the foster father molested her. To this day, after five years, this loving, caring blood-relative grandmother does not even have visitation privileges with the children. The little girls are, in my opinion, permanently traumatized, and the young mother of the girls was so traumatized with shock when the girls were first removed from her that she has not recovered. Throughout this case and through the process of dealing with multiple other mismanaged cases of the Department of Family and Children Services (DFCS), I have worked with other desperate parents and children across the state because they have no rights and no one with whom to turn. I have witnessed ruthless behavior from many caseworkers, social workers, investigators, lawyers, judges, therapists, and others, such as those who "pick up" the children. I have been stunned by what I have seen and heard from victims all over the state of Georgia. In this report, I am focusing on the Georgia Department of Family and Children's Services (DFCS). However, I believe Child Protective Services nationwide has become corrupt and that the entire system is broken almost beyond repair. I am convinced parents and families should be warned of the dangers. The Department of Child Protective Services, known as the Department of Family and Children Service (DFCS) in Georgia and other titles in other states, has become a "protected empire" built on taking children and separating families. This is not to say that there are not those children who do need to be removed from wretched situations and need protection.

This report is concerned with the children and parents caught up in "legal kidnapping," ineffective policies, and DFCS, which does not remove a child or children when a child is enduring torment and abuse. (See Exhibit A and Exhibit B)

In one county in my District, I arranged a meeting for thirty-seven families to speak freely and without fear. These poor parents and grandparents spoke of their painful, heart-wrenching encounters with DFCS. Their suffering was overwhelming. They wept and cried. Some did not know where their children were and had not seen them in years. I had witnessed the "Gestapo" at work, and I witnessed the deceitful conditions under which children were taken in the middle of the night, out of hospitals, off of school buses, and out of homes.

In one county, a private drug testing business was operating within the DFCS department that required many, many drug tests from parents and individuals for profit. In another county, children were not removed when they were enduring the worst possible abuse.

Due to being exposed, several employees in a particular DFCS office were fired. However, they have now been rehired either in neighboring counties or in the same county again.

According to the calls I am now receiving, the conditions in that county are returning to the same practices that they had before the light was shown on their deeds. Having worked with probably 300 cases statewide, I am convinced there is no responsibility and no accountability in the system. I have come to the conclusion:

- *that poor parents oftentimes are targeted to lose their children because they do not have the where-with all to hire lawyers and fight the system. Being poor does not mean you are not a good parent or that you do not love your child, or that your child should be removed and placed with strangers;*

- *that all parents are capable of making mistakes and that making a mistake does not mean your children are always to be removed from the home. Even if the home is not perfect, it is home; and that's where a child is the safest and where he or she wants to be, with family;*

- *that parenting classes, anger management classes, counseling referrals, therapy classes, and on and on are demanded of parents with no compassion by the system even while they are at work and while their children are separated from them. This can take months or even years, and it emotionally devastates both children and parents. Parents are victimized by "the system" that makes a profit for holding children longer and "bonuses" for not returning children;*

- *that caseworkers and social workers are often times guilty of fraud. They withhold evidence. They fabricate evidence, and they seek to terminate parental rights.*

- *However, when charges are made against them, the charges are ignored;*

- *that the separation of families is growing as a business because local governments have grown accustomed to having taxpayer dollars to balance their ever-expanding budgets;*

- *that Child Protective Service and Juvenile Court can always hide behind a confidentiality clause in order to protect their decisions and keep the funds flowing.*

- *There should be open records and "court watches"! Look who is being paid! There are state employees, lawyers, court investigators, court personnel, and judges.*

There are psychologists, psychiatrists, counselors, caseworkers, therapists, foster parents, adoptive parents, and on and on. All are looking to the children in state custody to provide job security. Parents do not realize that social workers are the glue that holds "the system" together that funds the court, the child's attorney, and multiple other jobs including DFCS's attorney.

That The Adoption and the Safe Families Act, set in motion by President Bill Clinton, offered cash "bonuses" to the states for every child they adopted out of foster care.

In order to receive the "adoption incentive bonuses," local child protective services need more children. They must have merchandise (children) that sell and you must have plenty of them so the buyer can choose. Some counties are known to give a $4,000 bonus for each child adopted and an additional $2,000 for a "special needs" child.

Employees work to keep the federal dollars flowing; that there is double dipping. The funding continues as long as the child is out of the home. When a child in foster care is placed with a new family, "adoption bonus funds" are available. When a child is placed in a mental health facility and is on 16 drugs per day, like two children of a constituent of mine, more funds are involved; that there are no financial resources and no real drive to unite a family and help keep them together; that the incentive for social workers to return children to their parents quickly after taking them has disappeared and who in protective services will step up to the plate and say, "This must end! No one, because they are all in the system together and a system with no leader and no clear policies will always fail the children. Look at the waste in government that is forced upon the taxpayer; that the "Policy Manual" is considered "the last word" for DFCS.

However, it is too long, too confusing, poorly written, and does not take the law into consideration; if the lives of children were improved by removing them from their homes, there might be a greater need for protective services, but today, all children are not always safer. Children, of whom I am aware, have been raped and impregnated in foster care, and the head of a Foster Parents Association in my District was recently arrested because of child molestation; some parents are even told if they want to see their children or grandchildren, they must divorce their spouse. Many, who are under privileged, feeling they have no option, will divorce and then just continue to live together. This is an antifamily policy, but parents will do anything to get their children home with them.

- *fathers, (non-custodial parents), I must add, are oftentimes treated as criminals without access to their own children and have child support payments strangling the very life out of them;*

- *that the Foster Parents Bill of Rights does not bring out that a foster parent is there only to care for a child until the child can be returned home. Many Foster Parents today use the Foster Parent Bill of Rights to hire a lawyer and seek to adopt the child from the real parents, who are desperately trying to get their child home and out of the system;*

- *that tax dollars are being used to keep this gigantic system afloat, yet the victims, parents, grandparents, guardians, and especially the children, are charged for the system's services.*

- *that grandparents have called from all over the State of Georgia trying to get custody of their grandchildren. DFCS claims relatives are contacted, but there are cases that prove differently. Grandparents who lose their grandchildren to strangers have lost their own flesh and blood. The children lose their family heritage, and grandparents and parents lose all connections to their heirs.*

- *that The National Center on Child Abuse and Neglect in 1998 reported that six times as many children died in foster care than in the general public and that once removed to official "safety", these children are far more likely to suffer abuse, including sexual molestation than in the general population.*

- *That according to the California Little Hoover*

- *Commission Report in 2003, 30% to 70% of the children in California group homes do not belong there and should not have been removed from their homes. Please continue. (See Final Remarks on the next page)*

Final Remarks

On my desk are scores of cases of exhausted families and troubled children. It has been beyond me to turn my back on these suffering, crying, and sometimes beaten down individuals. We are mistreating the most innocent. Child Protective Services have become adults centered to the detriment of children. No longer is judgment based on what the child needs or who the child wants to be with or what is really best for the whole family; it is some adult or bureaucrat who makes the decisions, based often on just hearsay, without ever consulting a family member, or just what is convenient, profitable, or less troublesome for a director of DFCS. I have witnessed such injustice and harm brought to these families that I am not sure if I even believe reform of the system is possible! The system cannot be trusted.

It does not serve the people. It obliterates families and children simply because it has the power to do so. Children deserve better. Families deserve better. It's time to pull back the curtain and set our children and families free.

"Speak up for those who cannot speak for themselves, for the rights of all who are destitute.

Speak up and judge fairly; defend the rights of the poor and the needy."

Proverbs

31:8-9

Please continue to read:

Recommendations

Exhibit A

Exhibit B

RECOMMENDATIONS

1. *Call for an Independent audit of the Department of Family and Children's Services (DFCS) to expose corruption and fraud.*
2. *Activate immediate change. Every day that passes means more families and children are subject to being held hostage.*

3. *End the financial incentives that separate families.*

4. *Grant to parents their rights in writing.*

5. *Mandate a search for family members to be given the opportunity to adopt their own relatives.*

6. *Mandate a jury trial where every piece of evidence is presented before removing a child from his or her parents.*

7. *Require a warrant or a positive emergency circumstance before removing children from their parents. (Judge Arthur G. Christean, Utah Bar Journal, January, 1997 reported that "except in emergency circumstances, including the need for immediate medical care, require warrants upon affidavits of probable cause before entry upon private property is permitted for the forcible removal of children from their parents.")*

8. *Uphold the laws when someone fabricates or presents false evidence. If a parent alleges fraud, hold a hearing with the right to discovery of all evidence. Senator Nancy Schaefer, 50th District of Georgia. Continue to Exhibit A on the next page.*

EXHIBIT A

December 5, 2006

Jeremy's Story

(Some names withheld due to future hearings)

As told to Senator Nancy Schaefer by Sandra (XXXX), a foster parent of Jeremy for 2 Vi years. My husband and I received Jeremy when he was 2 weeks old and we have been the only parents he has really ever known. He lived with us for 27 months. (XXXX) is the grandfather of Jeremy, and he is known for molesting his own children, for molesting Jeremy and has been court ordered not to be around Jeremy. (XXXX) is the mother of Jeremy, who has been diagnosed to be mentally ill, and also is known to have molested Jeremy. (XXXX) and Jeremy's uncle is a registered sex offender and (XXXX) is the biological father, who is a drug addict and alcoholic and who continues to be in and out of jail. Having just described Jeremy's world, all of these adults are not to be any part of Jeremy's life, yet for years DFCS has known that they are.

DFCS had to test (XXXX) (the grandfather) and his son (XXXX) (the uncle) and (XXXX) to determine the real father. (XXXX) is the biological father although any of them might have been. In court, it appeared from the case study, that everyone involved knew that this little boy had been molested by family members, even by his own mother, (XXXX). In court, (XXX), the mother of Jeremy, admitted to having had sex with (XXXX) (the grandfather) and (XXXX) (her own brother) that morning. Judge (XXXX) and DFCS gave Jeremy to his grandmother that same day. (XXXX), the grandmother, is over 300 lbs., is unable to drive, and is unable to take care of Jeremy due to physical problems. She also has been in a mental hospital several times due to her behavior.

Even though it was ordered by the court that the grandfather (XXXX), the uncle (XXXX) (a convicted sex offender), (XXXX) his mother who molested him and (XXXX) his biological father, a convicted drug addict, were not to have anything to do with the child, they all continue to come and go as they please at (XXXX address), where Jeremy has been "sentenced to live" for years. This residence has no bathroom and little heat. The front door and the windows are boarded. (See pictures) This home should have been condemned years ago. I have been in this home. No child should ever have to live like this or with such people. Jeremy was taken from us at age 2 Vi years after (XXXX) obtained attorney (XXXX), who was the same attorney who represented him in a large settlement from an auto accident. I am told, that attorney (XXXX), as grandfather's attorney, is known to have repeatedly gotten (XXXX) off of several criminal charges in White County.

This is a matter of record and is known by many in White County. I have copies of some records. (XXXX grandfather), through (XXXX attorney's) work, got (XXXX), the grandmother of Jeremy, legal custody of Jeremy. (XXXX grandfather) who cannot read or write also got his daughter (XXXX) and son

(XXXX) diagnosed by government agencies as mentallyill.(XXXX grandfather), through legal channels, has taken upon himself all control of the family and is able to take possession of any government funding coming to these people.

It was during this time that Jeremy was to have a six-month transitional period between (XXXX grandmother) and my family as we were to give him up. The court ordered agreement was to have been 4 days at our house and 3 days at (XXXX grandmother). DFCS stopped the visits within 2 weeks. The reason given by DFCS was the child was too traumatized going back and forth. In truth, Jeremy begged us and screamed never to be taken back to (XXXX his grandmother) house, which we have on video. We, as a family, have seen Jeremy in stores from time to time with (XXXX grandmother) and the very people he is not to be around. At each meeting Jeremy continues to run to us wherever he sees us and it is clear he is suffering. This child is in a desperate situation and this is why I am writing, and begging you Senator Schaefer, to do something on this child's behalf. Jeremy can clearly describe in detail his sexual molestation by every member of this family and this sexual abuse continues to this day.

When Jeremy was 5 years of age I took him to Dr. (XXXX) of Habersham County who did indeed agree that Jeremy's rectum was black and blue and the physical damage to the child was clearly a case of sexual molestation . Early in Jeremy's life, when he was in such bad physical condition, we took him to Egleston Children Hospital where at two months of age therapy was to begin three times a week. DFCS decided that the (XXXX grandparent family) should participate in his therapy. However, the therapist complained over and over that the (XXXX grandparent family) would not even wash their hands and would cause Jeremy to cry during these sessions. (XXXX the grandmother), after receiving custody no longer allowed the therapy because it was an inconvenience. The therapist reported that this would be a terrible thing to do to this child. Therapy was stopped and it was detrimental to the health of Jeremy.

During (XXXX grandmother) custody, (XXXX uncle) has shot

Jeremy with a BB gun and there is a report at (XXXX)

County Sheriff's office. There are several amber alerts at Cornelia Wal-Mart, Commerce Wal-Mart, and a 911 report from (XXXX) County SherifTs Department when Jeremy was lost. (XXXX grandmother), to teach Jeremy a lesson, took thorn bush limbs and beat the bottoms of his feet. Jeremy's feet got infected and his feet had to be lanced by Dr. (XXXX). Then Judy called me to pick him up after about 4 days to take him back to the doctor because of intense pain. I took Jeremy to Dr. (XXXX) in Gainesville. Dr. (XXXX) said surgery was needed immediately and a cast was added. After returning home, (XXXX), his grandfather and (XXXX), his uncle, took him into the hog lot and allowed him to walk in the filth. Jeremy's feet became so infected for a 2"** time that he was again taken back to Dr. (XXXX) and the hospital. No one in the hospital could believe this child's living conditions.

Jeremy is threatened to keep quiet and not say anything to anyone. I have videos, reports, arrest records and almost anything you might need to help Jeremy. Please call my husband, Wendell, or me at any time. Sandra and (XXXX) husband (XXXX)

Continue - Exhibit B

Failure of DFCS to remove six desperate children A brief report regarding six children that Habersham County DFCS director failed to remove as disclosed to Senator Nancy Schaefer by Sheriff Deray Fincher of Habersham County. Sheriff

Deray Fincher, Chief of Police Don Ford and Chief Investigator, Lt. Greg Bowen Chief called me to meet with them immediately, which I did on Tuesday, October 16, 2007 Sheriff Fincher, after contacting the Director of Habersham County DFCS several times to remove six children from being horribly abused, finally had to get a court order to remove the children himself with the help of two police officers. The children, four boys and two girls, were not just being abused; they were being tortured by a monster father. The six children and a live-in girlfriend were terrified of this man, the abuser. The children never slept in a bed, but always on the floor. The place where they lived was unfit for human habitation. The father on one occasion hit one of the boys across his head with a bat and cut the boy's head open. The father then proceeded to hold the boy down and sew up the child's head with a needle and red thread. However, even with beatings and burnings, this is only a fraction of what the father did to these children and to the live-in girlfriend. Sheriff Fincher has pictures of the abuse and condition of one of the boys and at the writing of this report, he has the father in jail in Habersham County. It should be noted that when the DFCS director found out that Sheriff Fincher was going to remove the children, she called the father and warned him to flee. This is not the only time this DFCS director failed to remove a child when she needed to do so.

(See Exhibit A)

The egregious acts and abhorrent behavior of officials who are supposed to protect children can no longer be tolerated. Senator Nancy Schaefer SO'' District of Georgia Senator Nancy*

Schaefer 302 B Coverdell Office Building 1 8 Capitol Square, SW Atlanta, Georgia 30334 Phone: 404-463-1367 Fax: 404-657-3217

Senator Nancy Schaefer, District Office. P.O. Box 294, Turnerville, Georgia 30580

Stories from families who have been affected by Child Protective Services

Grandparents Fight Against DHR Through The Mercy And Grace Of God (The Struggles To Gain Grandparents Rights)

An Alabama couple is frightened that they may never see their granddaughters Sarah and Katie again and is concerned about their well-being. They need to be with their maternal grandparents, where they should have been back in September 2012.

This all started on September 21, 2012, with the DHR (the state's child protective services) when they removed our granddaughters, Sarah and Katie from their home where their mom (Faith Smith), the guy friend (James or Jim Dean), and his mom (Rhonda Dean) lived in Adger, Alabama.

Sarah and Katie were placed in a foster home about 30 minutes from their other home. The foster home already had 7 people in the home. We did not know they had been removed until about a week or two later when we got a phone call from the first DHR case worker (Angi Collins). If we had known we would have been at the court date on Sept 24, 2012 but we had no idea. This is when we starting getting to visit with the girls. The first time was on a weekend at the foster parents (Tim and Dee Pearce) home which is in Adger, Alabama. We have passed all the requirements that DHR wanted. This is when DHR should have placed the granddaughters with the grandparents, which is family, but DHR did not do their job in the reunification of family like they are supposed to.

On November 5, 2012, we had an ISP for the girls. The case worker (Angi Collins) called them (parents) out on so many lies, and the foster dad (Tim Pearce) did the same. Then the guy friend (Jim Dean) and his mom (Rhonda Dean) were making the mom of our daughter (Faith Smith) speak up and tell lies about her dad (Brent Smith) and what he did to her when she was 5 or 8. We had two other daughters living in the home. The middle child was 18 years old, and the youngest was 16 years old. Our 18-year-old told the first case worker (Angi Collins) if something did happen, would I still be living in the home? Also, why didn't DHR remove the 16-year-old and the exchange student for further investigation of these false accusations that she (Faith) was forced into bringing up in the ISP meeting on November 5, 2012?

November 27, 2012 was a court date we attended and found out the case worker (Angi Collins) was sick and could not make it but then found out a week later that she had been called off the case for some reason and there would be a new case worker who would be in contact with us. We were contacted by mail in December 2012 by the new case worker (Latesia Jefferson) and then again in January 2013 about the date for the ISP for the girls. The Bio parent filed a police report on December 12, 2012. She waited a month and 7 days before she filed a false police report about these accusations that she brought up at the ISP on November 5, 2012.

The second case worker (Latesia Jefferson) passed us with all the requirements that we had to have with DHR. Also, we have passed the CASA and an Assistant from DHR requirements for the girls. All of them have said we are ready for them to come live with us, the grandparents. The first case aide also said, let's bring those girls home where they belong. One time in court in the year 2013, one of the lawyers said to the judge, "Your honor, if we had any place to put the kids outside of DHR, we would." Okay, what are we? Chopped liver?

We have had about 6 backgrounds since all this mess with DHR started in September 2012 because we have had international exchange students living with us for the school year, have worked with children's camps with a foster care agency, and vacation Bible School with our church. Plus, my husband has to have FBI checks and fingerprint checks for his job.

We had a recent background check in July 2015 and again in August 2015, and all came back clear, and we still do not have our granddaughters. I just had a background check done in May 2016 and a child neglect/abuse check done, too, and they came out clear again. So, about 10 background checks and child neglect/abuse checks have been done since 2012, and still NO granddaughters. The last time we had visits with our granddaughters was June 9, 2013.

Before the visit started, we noticed that the oldest (Sarah) had bruises on her legs and a scratch on her arm that looked infected. So we told the new case aide about them and showed her, too. Then, two weeks later, our visits were terminated. The case worker said that they had an ISP meeting on June 18, 2013, that we did not know about, and since the parents were still parents, they did not want us to see the girls. It's kind of funny that they had an ISP a week after our visit with the girls. Wonder what the new case aide wrote in her report that day.

However, DHR was there to reunify children with family members. So far, they have not done their job in reunifying the children with family who have been waiting for 4 years. They have passed all the requirements not just once but 4 times by 4 different DHR workers and passed a lot of background checks and still NO granddaughters.

There was a court date that was supposed to be on August 24, 2015, at 8:30 am, but the only people who showed up were our lawyer, me, and our two bio daughters. After being there about an hour our lawyer told us that they were splitting the dates up for the children. Whatever that means sounds kind of fishy to us. Through all these years, we have been treated like the bad guys and the parents and the other grandparents the good guys. December 2, 2015, was court again for our granddaughters, but nothing happened since their criminal case is still pending. WOW. It's so sad that DHR is doing these children like they are when there is a good family that loves them and can care for them. June 1, 2016 was court again for our granddaughters and again nothing happened since their criminal case is still pending.

How can we get it through their (DHR) thick skull that we have done nothing wrong and Sarah and Katie NEED to be with a family that has passed the requirements by DHR four (4) times? On September 14, 2016, this time, we went to court for grandparents' visits with Sarah and Katie, but the judge denied it and did not give a reason why it was denied. She (the judge) did not want to hear anything, not even from the GAL or the CASA. They wanted answers too. For once, they (GAL and CASA) were on our side but the judge did not want to hear anything. We missed their first steps, their first words, their first tooth, and their first time eating table food. Missed out on Sarah's first day of Kindergarten in August 2016.

Sarah' first homecoming week of 2016. We might have missed Sarah first loose tooth and the first visit from the tooth fairy. What other first are we as grandparents going to miss with our granddaughters. December 7, 2016: Again, we went to court to get grandparents visits with Sarah and Katie, and again, the court continued. How long is DHR going to keep our granddaughters in their care. This corruption has gone on for 4 years too long. This was also when we found out there was a third grandchild named Hunter, who was born in 2014. Now, all this makes sense as to why our visits were terminated in June 2013 because Faith was pregnant and starting to show and did not want us to know about the child. Plus, DHR was trying to cover its tracks in the corruption of the system. This is legal kidnapping.

September 19, 2017: Again, we went to court for some petitions that we had submitted for becoming parties, visits and custody and again they were thrown out. When is this going to end? This corruption NEEDS TO END... Judge — Lorraine Pringle, GAL — Lori Frasure.

Articles On Child Sex Trafficking The Media Won't Tell You About.

Medical Kidnapping

December 3, 2018, by Brian Shilhavy, Editor, Health Impact News

800,000 children a year in the United States go missing, many of them being sexually trafficked through pedophilia networks where the children suffer unimaginable horrors such as Satanic ritual abuse. This number is comprised of documented cases of children gone missing, and does not include children who are born and bred into pedophilia networks and have no birth certificates, or undocumented immigrant children who come across the borders.

Philadelphia CPS Tries to Silence Grandmother Exposing Rape of Grandchild in DHS Foster Care

Commentary by Terri LaPoint Health Impact News

Child Protective Services, funded by American taxpayers, doesn't believe that they should be held accountable to the citizens who foot the bill. Repeatedly, we have seen efforts by various state CPS agencies around the country to silence parents who speak out about the abuse that they and their children suffer at the hands of social workers and courts, as well as abuse that happens to their children in foster homes, group homes, and hospitals. CPS social workers and their attorneys sometimes request, and judges approve, gag orders demanding that families keep quiet about what they have seen. Not content with the violation of the parents' Constitutional First Amendment rights, social workers frequently retaliate against family members who talk, pushing for quicker termination of parental rights, denying visitation, or making up new fictitious allegations. The story we share today plays out in CPS cases every single day all over the county. If Philadelphia Department of Human Services (DHS) has their way, the story will disappear and no one will hear about it.

Richard Wexler of the National Coalition for Child Protection Reform (NCCPR) asks for the help of our readers to make sure that the story doesn't disappear. He published this blog piece on Tuesday, November 27, 2018: There is a news story that Philadelphia's child welfare agency desperately does not want the world to read. What do you think we should do about that?

Reporter P.J. D'Annunzio of the *Legal Intelligencer* has written a series of articles about "the horror show that is foster care in Philadelphia." The first article (Link) delved into exposing abuse that happens to children at the hands of the state once they are taken from their families and placed into foster care in Philadelphia. D'Annunzio opened with the story of grandmother Virginia McKale of New Jersey learning to her horror that her 9-year-old grandson in Philadelphia DHS foster care had been raped by another foster child. She had previously petitioned the court for custody of her grandchildren, and she had plenty of room in her 7-bedroom home. However: ...*former Philadelphia Family Court Judge Lyris Younge denied that request because*

McKale lives across state lines. (Source) Judge Younge has since been removed from the

Family Court bench. See: Philadelphia Family Court Judge Exposed and Charged with Illegal Medical Kidnapping

According to NCCPR: *The younger child, who suffers from severe brain damage, was institutionalized. The older child, age 9, was moved five different times. In the fourth of those placements he was raped by another child. The story was careful to use pseudonyms to protect the children's identifies.*

"They know they've done wrong," McKale told the Legal Intelligencer "and every time I turn around they're trying to cover it up." McKale had no idea how right she was. An agency with a shred of decency would have placed the children with their grandmother and surrounded the family with all the support they needed to heal from what the agency itself, and its private contractors, did to them. Needless to say, that was not the response from the Philadelphia Department of Human Services. Instead, DHS got a judge to issue two orders: First, a gag order, so McKale can't tell anyone any more about what DHS and its contractors have done or are doing to her family.

Retaliation

As happens in many CPS cases, Virginia McKale faced retaliation in the form of visitation with her grandchildren being restricted. NCCPR continues: *Even worse, they got an order rescinding unsupervised visits. Now all visits must be under the supervision of the very agencies she's criticized — so you can be sure McKale will be under a microscope as the visit supervisors search for excuses to cut off visits all together. At a minimum it will ratchet up the stress all around and make visits harder to schedule. So in effect, Philadelphia is punishing a nine-year-old rape victim because his grandmother dared to speak out about how he was raped in foster care.* See more about the gag order and retaliation in the *Legal Intelligencer:* Court Silences Woman Who

Spoke Out About Grandchild's Abuse in Philadelphia Foster Care How You Can Help

Richard Wexler of NCCPR calls for the public to take to social media and let everyone know what is happening to this family and to countless others: *...there is one thing we can do about this: Make the gag order backfire. I almost never explicitly urge people to do anything on social media — partly because it angers the social media gods. But this once, I think an exception is called for. The Legal Intelligencer published a story that the Philadelphia Department of Human Services desperately does not want the world to see. So let's do everything in our power to make sure as much of the world as possible sees it!* He concludes with this: *So, we know that the one thing DHS really cares about is not the children or the families — it's not having its failings exposed to the world. What should we do about that?*

Indiana High Court Accuses CPS of "Significant Violations of Due Process in

Termination of Parental Rights" **Commentary by Terri LaPoint**

Health Impact News

Cracks are starting to be exposed in the foundation of the state sponsored child kidnapping structure of Child "Protective" Services. Parents who have been fighting the system for their children have seen these gaping flaws all along, but for decades anyone with power to change it has turned a blind eye to their plight.

Finally, it appears that the higher courts in one state are beginning to recognize that the system is, indeed, violating parental rights with alarming frequency. Appellate judges from the Indiana Court of Appeals recently sent a strong rebuke to the Department of Child Services (DCS), citing "significant violations of due process occurring in termination of parental rights cases throughout the state." *Indianapolis NBC affiliate Channel 13* reports that the judges acknowledged that there is a pattern of "repeated violations" of parental and Constitutional due process rights by DCS. While the fact that the agency routinely violates parents' rights certainly comes as no surprise to anyone on the front lines of the battle, the admission by the appeals court and by DCS itself that it is happening comes as a shock, albeit a good one, to attorneys and parents alike.

13 Investigates: DCS violated parents' rights and took kids away: Could this be the beginning of the dominoes falling? Will other states take notice and follow suit? Bob Segall of NBC 13 writes: *The Court of*

Appeals cited a "disturbing trend" with 10 cases it received between September 2017 and March of this year. In each of the cases, one or more parents appealed the termination of their rights, and DCS asked for the case to be sent back to the trial court rather than have the appellate judges issue a ruling. In a July court order, the Court of Appeals formally admonished DCS. The judges wrote, "DCS essentially concedes that [the parent appealing the termination] has either not been provided with adequate notice or that their due process rights have been violated." The judges criticized DCS for repeatedly requesting that the cases be returned to a lower court rather than submitting a formal response to the appeals, thereby avoiding DCS having to defend its actions. The Court of Appeals also took aim at the trial courts, reminding judges that they too have a "duty to ensure that litigants' due process rights are not violated." In its most recent opinion, the judges were so frustrated by "repeated violations" of the parent's rights and other failures of the trial court, they wrote, Public Defender Stunned at Turn of Events *We are at a loss as to any possible, just reason for such conduct.* Stephanie Thomas is an Indiana mother with mental health issues and a drug addiction history. Her daughter was placed into foster care in 2016. She learned in July that her parental rights had been terminated. DCS had held the hearing without notifying her: *I never got papers. I never got any notice. The only thing I got was a text after the hearing…. the case worker wouldn't talk to me any more and said 'your rights have been terminated.* She immediately filed for an appeal and was assigned public defender Dorothy Ferguson.

According to *NBC 13 Investigates*, the attorney "immediately recognized problems with the way in which DCS handled the case." Nonetheless, as parents from all over America can attest, it was not unusual for DCS/CPS to violate their own policies and the law when taking children from their parents. In fact, dozens of people from many different states have told *Health Impact News* that they were told that "the Constitution doesn't apply in family court," as they watched all semblance of due process and Constitutional principles dissipate before their very eyes. Ferguson still believed that they had "a good chance of winning the appeal." What happened next was nothing short of amazing.

NBC 13 Investigates reports:

Thomas' attorney then received a surprise phone call from the Indiana Attorney General's office. She discovered the AG, who represents state agencies such as DCS, was also concerned by DCS's actions and wanted to help her client. "They told me they agreed with our position and wanted to file a motion to send the case back to the trial court," recalled Ferguson. "I was like 'What? This is crazy!' This has never happened to me in my entire [career]. That's really unheard of."

DCS Director Agrees with Appeals Court Terry J. Stigdon, MSN, RN, was appointed by Indiana governor Eric Holcomb in late 2017 to take over the position of director of the state's troubled DCS agency. The governor called for a review of the DCS department in partnership with the Child Welfare Policy and Practice Group. DCS director Terry Stigdon admits that the DCS department is not doing well.

According to *FOX 59 News*, Stigdon began her career working at the local children's hospital as a pediatric intensive care nurse in 1998. At the time of her appointment, she was the "clinical director of operations at Riley Hospital for Children at IU Health in Indianapolis— overseeing strategy, finance, personnel, research and programs for several of the hospital's key divisions, including emergency, trauma and nursing."

After the Indiana Court of Appeals rendered their decision on almost a dozen cases, in which they found the department to be violating many parental rights, DCS director Terry Stigdon issued a statement to *NBC 13 Investigates*: *After a thorough review of the cases in question, I believe our legal work has fallen short of the standards I have set for our agency. We are working to recruit and retain top legal talent and provide additional staff training…. as well as build and maintain strong relationships with judges across Indiana.*

Riley Hospital Child Abuse Pediatricians Responsible for Multiple Medical

Kidnappings The director's previous employer, Riley Children's Hospital, has been involved with every *Medical Kidnap* case in the state of Indiana that we have covered previously. The hospital employs Child Abuse Pediatricians Dr. Roberta Hibbard and Dr. Shannon

Thompson, both of whom accused parents of abuse instead of figuring out that the children had metabolic bone conditions which led to their broken bones.

Laura Gellinger and Dylan Day actually spent time in prison for "abuse" of their baby after Dr. Roberta Hibbard from Riley Hospital and Dr. Jamie Brummett of Reid Hospital said that x-rays showed multiple broken bones. The baby showed all the classic signs of metabolic bone disease, but the doctors refused to test for them. Baby Jackson was adopted out. See their story:

- Indiana Parents Lose Their Baby and 2 Years of Their Lives in Jail for "Abuse" They Say Never Happened

- **Nikki and Rodney Wisler were arrested for accusations of abusing their baby. Dr. Roberta Hibbard said that baby Leigh Ann had a broken tibia, but when medical expert Dr. Ayoub said that there was no fracture on the x-ray, she retracted her diagnosis. See their story:**

- Indiana Parents' Trip to E.R. Results in Children Kidnapped – Names Slandered in Local Media – Lives Ruined **Child Abuse Pediatrician Dr. Roberta Hibbard of Riley Children's Hospital. Photo source. • Austin and Andrea Timmons had their boys seized by DCS after Dr. Shannon Thompson found fractures in their youngest son and accused the parents of abuse. Other doctors later** figured out that the baby had metabolic bone disease and Ehlers-Danlos Syndrome. The other doctors also could not find the rib fractures that Dr. Thompson had diagnosed. See their story:

- Two Indiana Boys Medically Kidnapped Remain in CPS Custody Despite Testimony of Medical Experts

- Ally Allen and John Kremitzki were accused of abuse when Dr. Shannon Thompson diagnosed multiple fractures in their first son. The whites of his eyes had a blue tint, and he had other classic signs of osteogenesis imperfecta and other metabolic bone disease. Dr. Ayoub diagnosed infantile rickets. The couple's youngest son was taken when he was born, because DCS already had custody of his brother. Dr. Thompson reportedly showed the court an x-ray of their son, only it wasn't him. The x-ray belonged to another child. See their story:

- Indiana Couple Loses over 2 Years of Their Babies' Lives because of Testimony of "Child Abuse Specialist"Child Abuse Pediatrician Dr. Shannon Thompson. Photo source.

- Jade and Lehla Jerger had their little girl taken away from them after Riley Children's Hospital got involved. The toddler was having up to 100 seizures a day with conventional medical treatment with Keppra, a dangerous drug with many side effects. When the Jergers started treating her with CBD oil from hemp, the results were almost miraculous, but doctors at Riley called DCS and insisted that she be taken off of the CBD oil and put back on Keppra. See their story:

- Medical Tyranny: Indiana Hospital and CPS Force Parents to Give Toddler Dangerous Drug After Seeking Second Opinion **Only 15% of the allegations against Indiana families are substantiated by the Department of Child Services. See:** 85% of Reports to Indiana Child Protective Services Unsubstantiated – Families Destroyed Needlessly

How Many More? Indiana public defender Dorothy Ferguson asked a question when she was being interviewed by *NBC 13 Investigates*: *How many other cases are out there without proper due process?* The answer is – too many, not only in Indiana. Denial of due process is not the exception with Child or Adult Protective Services all across the nation. It is the norm. After four years of investigating cases of medical kidnappings of children and adults from Massachusetts to California and everywhere in between, it is clear that families are routinely denied basic human and Constitutional rights when it comes to the seizure of family members by the state. The right to be secure in one's home, to be free from search and seizure without a warrant, and the right to familial attachment, in addition to the right to due process, are being denied to hundreds of thousands of American families every single year.

The Indiana Appeals Court judges cites the Indiana Supreme Court case *In re Adoption of* O.R. 16 N.E.3d 965, 972 (Ind. 2014), noting that: *the Fourteenth Amendment to the United States Constitution protects the rights of parents to establish a home and raise their children, that parents have a fundamental liberty interest in the care custody and control of their children, and that the parent-child relationship is one of the most valued relationships in our culture.*

The Troxel vs. Granville case before the Supreme Court of the United States of America clarified that: *the Due Process Clause of the Fourteenth Amendment protects the fundamental right of parents to make decisions concerning the care, custody, and control of their children.* Yet, children, disabled adults, and senior citizens alike are being taken from their homes, sometimes permanently, based on false allegations, lies by social workers, misdiagnoses by (or egos of) doctors, or exaggerations of parental shortcomings that the same system has no problem with in foster parents. Tennessee attorney and family advocate Connie Reguli calls it "generational genocide."

You have read about how it went from the INDIGENOUS people being kidnapped and sold, to African people being bought and sold, to our children and agents receiving "bonuses", all as Adolf Hitler said in his speech, "The state must declare the child to be the most precious treasure of the people. As long as the government is perceived as working for the benefit of the children, the people will happily endure almost any curtailment of liberty and almost any deprivation." The question is: WHOSE CHILD IS IT? YOURS OR THE GOVERNMENTS?

In the article National Study Faults Federal "Adoption & Safe Families Act" for Consigning Children to Permanent Separation from Parents September 7, 2006, Lynn Lu, Brennan Center for Justice (212) 992-8645 Patricia Allard, Brennan Center for Justice (212) 998-6740, they go into detail about this very act: "WASHINGTON, D.C. Child welfare policies are colliding with the increasing incarceration of parents, primarily for low-level drug crimes, to tear families apart according to a policy report released today at a meeting of the Congressional Black Caucus by the Brennan Center for Justice at NYU School of Law.

The report, Rebuilding Families, Reclaiming Lives, faults the federal Adoption & Safe Families Act for unintentionally expediting the permanent separation of children from incarcerated parents. Under the 1997 law, states are required to terminate the parental rights of children who have been foster care for 15 of the last 22 months, subject to limited exceptions.

This report shows a painful unintended consequence of federal law. Far too many children are at risk of being permanently separated from their mothers whose worst crime may be drug addiction, said Michael Waldman, executive director of the Brennan Center. Congress should pass the Second Chance Act and give states support in their efforts to keep families together. The report finds that the median sentence imposed by state courts for non-violent drug offenses is 36 months too long to prevent a child without substitute care from being permanently removed from an incarcerated parents' custody under federal law.

Between 1990 and 2000, the number of minor children with an incarcerated mother nearly doubled. Today more than 1.5 million minors have a parent in prison. Drug offenses are the number one reason for maternal incarceration. Latina and African American women are more likely than any other group of people to be in prison for a non-violent drug offense. As a result, black children are more than nine times more likely than white children to have a parent in prison. The federal child welfare law is sentencing tens of thousands of children to life without a mother, stated Patricia Allard, a lawyer at the Brennan Center and co-author of the study.

The report calls on Congress to relax the timeline for termination of parental rights mandated by the Adoption & Safe Families Act and to consider alternatives like subsidized legal guardianship to keep families together.

The report also urges states to end barriers to family reunification. Most moms in state and federal prisons are held more than 100 miles away from their children. Prisons are often far away from public transportation, and communicating in between visits is often extremely difficult, stated Lynn Lu, a lawyer at the Brennan Center and co-author of the report.

The study calls on states to coordinate between prison and child welfare officials to keep families together. We need to recognize that, for now, the prison system and the child welfare system are inextricably linked. States need to do a better job of keeping the bonds strong between children and an incarcerated parent, said Lu.

Rep. Sheila Jackson Lee (D-Texas) joined the Brennan Center in releasing the report. Rep. Jackson Lee is one of 112 sponsors of the Second Chance Act, a bipartisan bill that would help incarcerated individuals re-enter society with adequate support to become productive members of their communities.

Working with the Brennan Center, Rep. Jackson Lee has introduced an amendment to the House version of the Second Chance Act that would mandate the federal government coordinate with states to collect and disseminate information about best practices to maintain the bonds between incarcerated parents and children in foster care.

Corrections officials and child welfare officials need to work together to ensure that we protect the bonds between a child and her mother while she's incarcerated. I am hopeful that this report will strengthen our resolve to act on the Second Chance Act before this Congress adjourns, stated Rep. Jackson Lee.

The Brennan Center study calls on state reunification services to include affordable and accessible telephone communication, child-appropriate visiting rooms in prisons, facilitation of parents' participation in case planning for the future of their children, drug and alcohol rehabilitation, and opportunities for parental self-improvement.

Some states have taken affirmative steps to address the special needs of families with incarcerated parents and children in foster care, even in the absence of federal guidance. Specifically, the authors singled out California and New York as two states that have policies directly addressing the needs of foster children and their incarcerated parents.

In addition to New York and California, the authors praised Massachusetts for encouraging child welfare agencies to work in cooperation with incarcerated parents to promote a healthy relationship with their children and to avoid permanent separation. Currently, state officials in Hawaii, Missouri, New Mexico, Oregon, and Washington have taken steps to set up Task Forces between corrections and child welfare officials to develop plans to keep families together during and after the incarceration of a parent.

We found that several states recognize the importance of assisting incarcerated parents and their children in preserving their relationships where reunification is a real possibility and expressly require child welfare agencies to tailor services to the needs of these families, said Allard. The federal government needs to fix the Adoption and Safe Families Act to ensure that all states do the same.

As you have read from the report by late Georgia State Senator Nancy Schaefer, bonuses are paid to CPS agents when they remove children from the home.

How many more families will be destroyed? How many children's lives have been turned upside down, with parents being told that it is in **"the best interest of children"?**

In *Shattered Bonds: The Color of Child Welfare* (2002), Dorothy Roberts (Roberts, a professor of law at Northwestern University, argues that ASFA is a wrong-headed assault on family preservation that goes far beyond its goal of ensuring children's safety and establishes "a preference for adoption as the means of reducing the exploding foster care population.")

Ms. Roberts states why this act needs to be changed- "In the past several years, the pendulum of child welfare philosophy has swung decisively in the opposite direction. Congress has abandoned the focus on preventive and reunification programs it once expressed. Leading the way is the Adoption and Safe Families Act enacted by Congress in 1997 to amend the 1980 Child Welfare Act.6 President Clinton signed the law within a year of directing the federal government to take steps to double the number of foster children adopted annually to 54,000 by 2002.7 The new federal adoption law -- known as "ASFA" -- represents a dramatic change in the way the federal government deals with the overloaded foster care system. Its orientation has shifted from emphasizing the reunification of children in foster care with their biological families toward support for the adoption of these children into new families." DID I READ THAT CORRECT?

"President Clinton signed the law within a year of directing the federal government to take steps to double the number of foster children adopted annually to 54,000 by 2002."

DOUBLING THE NUMBER OF CHILDREN IN FOSTER CARE? So, Bill Clinton and his wife, Hillary, are responsible for giving CPS "teeth" to LEGALLY KIDNAP our children.

Is CPS Constitutional? According to Nancy Schaefer, the answer is NO!!! NEED PROOF? Let's LOOK AT AN INTERVIEW with Alex Jones and see what she said about CPS.

Nancy Schaefer's Interview

Less than a year before she was murdered, Nancy Schaefer appeared on the Jones Alex show to discuss the American foster care and adoption business, and the terrible corruption involved with it, including "bounties" on children and child se trafficking. Her interview is available via YouTube.

Par

Excerpts

Nancy Schaefer says that CPS is unconstitutional.

Parents across this country need to be warned of the dangers of Child Protection Services nationwide.

"The Department of Child Protective Services has become a protected empire. It' built on taking children and separating families."

After she lost her State Senate seat due to what she believes was her report onCPS, she began to talk to other State Representatives and Senators around the country who were being confronted with

CPS issues in their district, but they told her that if they did anything, they would lose their jobs just as Nancy Schaefer had.

Alex Jones asked her if there were "bounties on the heads of children" and Mrs. Schaefer said "yes," and that in fact just the day before she had learned that "an order" had come in to a CPS office stating what kind of child someone wanted to adopt.

Mrs. Schaefer states that the financial motive for the State to legally kidnap children was put in place in 1974 by Walter Mondale with the "Adoption and Safe Families Act." This was later expanded by President Bill Clinton in 1997 with The Adoption and Safe Families Act that gave states cash bonuses for every child adopted out of foster care. (Editor's note: Bill Clinton signed this bill into law, but the bill was passed by the Republican-led House and Senate led by Newt Gingrich, so it was a bi-partisan effort initiated by a Republican majority in Congress.)

Part 2

Excerpts:

In this segment, Mrs. Schaefer talks about how States have a "base formula" regarding how much each child is worth in terms of collecting federal funding, and how they can increase that formula to get all the federal funding that is available. If they get close to the end of the year and they have not collected all the funds available for that State, there is more incentive to put more children into foster care.

Mrs. Schaefer explained how the words "in the best interest of the child" have been redefined by CPS, whose goal is to destroy the family. She explained how grandparents often cannot even get custody of their own grandchildren when it would be in the best interest of the children to be with their grandparents. She explained how children are much more likely to be abused in foster care than they are when they are left with "abusive" parents.

She gives first hand experience of a case in her district where two little girls were removed from their mother because the mother allegedly had an unopened can of beer in her car, and the girls were placed into a foster home with many other children where they were sexually abused, including by the CPS caseworker who lived in the foster home.

Part 3

Excerpts:

In this third segment, Mrs. Schaefer finishes the story of how she became exposed to the corruption in CPS, with a grandmother in Florida who was trying to get custody of her grandchildren in Georgia, which is the story started in the previous section. She persisted with the help of Senator Schaefer, and eventually was able to get custody of her grandchildren, but then the juvenile court judge issued an order for the girls to become the custody of their biological father who lived on the West Coast, but had never been a part of their lives. He reportedly was in the business of "Adult Entertainment," which included pornography according to Mrs. Schaefer.

Both Alex Jones and Senator Schaefer comment on how many pedophiles are involved in social services like CPS working with children.

Mrs. Schaefer again reiterates that the system has to be exposed and completely dissolved. All federal funding needs to be cut off, and the rescuing of truly abused children in homes needs to become the function of law enforcement, and not social workers. This would provide due process of law. This mantra of hers to cut off funding and expose everything certainly provided a motive for someone to not want her doing that job.

One of the tragic things Mrs. Schaefer said in this segment was that she was overwhelmed with calls from families losing their children all across the U.S., and they had nowhere to turn for justice. "There is nowhere to go," she stated. This reflects our own experience here at MedicalKidnap.com since launching this website. Part 4

In this last segment, Alex Jones asked the Senator how to fight this corruption. Mrs. Schaefer replied that she tried to pass a bill in Georgia that would have helped to stop it, but it was defeated. She mentioned the incredible bureaucracy that exists in the system and all the jobs that "child protection services" provided, which is a huge "business."

So, as you can see, this problem goes back to the 1660s and continues to this day. Also, people who try to reveal this corruption never get a chance to tell the full story.

Case in point.

Jeffrey Epstein. He was a "friend" of Bill and Hillary Clinton.

https://en.wikipedia.org/wiki/Main_Page

Investigation:

Epstein's removal from suicide watch so soon after he was found with injuries to his neck, and in such a high-security federal facility, left some prison experts "stunned and angry".[229]

Attorney General Barr ordered an investigation by the Department of Justice Inspector General in addition to the investigation by the Federal Bureau of Investigation, saying that he was "appalled" by Epstein's death in federal custody.[11][230] Two days later Barr said there had been "serious irregularities" in the prison's handling of Epstein, promising "We will get to the bottom of what happened, and there will be accountability."[231]

In the evening before Epstein died, he was in good spirits according to a source familiar with Epstein's case.[232] Epstein told one of his lawyers before they left on Friday, the day before his death, that "I'll see you Sunday." Throughout his meetings with his lawyers, which occurred seven days a week and lasted up to 12 hours a day, he was positive. Epstein was confident that he was going to win the double-jeopardy motion in connection with his related 2008 Florida conviction. Epstein also had hope that on appeal that he would get bail. The appeal was pending before the US Second Circuit Court of Appeals at the time of his death.[232] On July 23, Epstein was found unconscious in his jail cell with injuries to his neck.[144] Epstein told his lawyers that his cellmate, the cop, had roughed him up.[232]

The national president of the Council of Prison Locals C-33, E. O. Young, stated that prisons "can't ever stop anyone who is persistent on killing themselves".[233] Between 2010 and 2016, around 124 inmates killed themselves while in federal custody, or around 20 prisoners per year, out of an inmate population of 180,000.[234][235] The last reported inmate suicide in the MCC facility in Manhattan was 21 years ago in 1998.[236] The union leader Young said it was unclear if there was video of Epstein's hanging or direct observations by jail officials. He said that while cameras are ubiquitous in the facility, he did not believe that the interior of inmates' cells were within their range. Young said union officials had long been raising concerns regarding staffing, as the Trump administration had imposed a hiring freeze and budget cuts on the BOP, adding "All this was caused by the administration."[233] President Serene Gregg, of the American Federation of Government Employees (AFGE) Local 3148, said MCC is functioning with fewer than 70 percent of the needed correctional officers, forcing many to work mandatory overtime and 60 to 70-hour workweeks.[233][237]

The White House did not respond to requests for comment. In previous congressional testimony, Attorney General Barr admitted the BOP was "short" about 4,000 to 5,000 employees. He had lifted the freeze and was working to recruit sufficient new officers to replace those who had departed.[233]

The circumstances surrounding the death quickly spawned conspiracy theories about Epstein's death,[238] with President Trump retweeting one suggesting that Bill Clinton was involved in causing Epstein's death

So, Bill Clinton, as president in 1997, signed the Adoption and Safe Families Act, strongly supported by Hillary Clinton, which gave Child Protective Services Judicial Authority over our children. Here is a current list of people who have died mysteriously that were associated with Bill and Hillary Clinton:

The Clinton Dead Pool

1. **James McDougal** – Clinton's convicted Whitewater partner, died of an apparent heart attack while in solitary confinement. He was a key witness in Ken Starr's investigation.

2. **Mary Mahoney** – A former White House intern, was murdered in July 1997 at a Starbucks Coffee Shop in Georgetown. The murder happened just after she was to go public with her story of sexual harassment in the White House.

3. 3 – **Vince Foster** – Former White House counselor and colleague of Hillary Clinton at Little Rock's Rose Law firm. They died of a gunshot wound to the head, which ruled a suicide.

4. 4 – **Ron Brown** – Secretary of Commerce and former DNC Chairman. Reported to have died by impact in a plane crash. A pathologist close to the investigation reported that there was a hole in the top of Brown's skull resembling a gunshot wound. At the time of his death, Brown was being investigated and spoke publicly of his willingness to cut a deal with prosecutors. The rest of the people on the plane also died. A few days later, the Air Traffic controller committed suicide.

5. **C. Victor Raiser, II** – Raiser, a major player in the Clinton fundraising organization, died in a private plane crash in July 1992.

6. **Paul Tulley** – Democratic National Committee Political Director, was found dead in a hotel room in Little Rock

in September 1992. Described by Clinton as a "dear friend and trusted advisor."

7. **Ed Willey** – Clinton fundraiser, found dead November 1993 deep in the woods in

8. VA of a gunshot wound to the head. Ruled a suicide. Ed Willey died on the same day his wife Kathleen Willey claimed Bill Clinton groped her in the Oval Office in the White House. Ed Willey was involved in several Clinton fundraising events.

9. **Jerry Parks** – Head of Clinton's gubernatorial security team in Little Rock. Gunned down in his car at a deserted intersection outside Little Rock Park, his son said his father was building a dossier on Clinton. He allegedly threatened to reveal this information. After he died, the files were mysteriously removed from his house.

10. **James Bunch** – Died from a gunshot suicide. It was reported that he had a "Black Book" of people, which contained names of influential people who visited prostitutes in Texas and Arkansas

11. **James Wilson** – Was found dead in May 1993 from an apparent hanging suicide. He was reported to have ties to Whitewater.

12. **Kathy Ferguson** – Ex-wife of Arkansas Trooper Danny Ferguson was found dead in May 1994 in her living room

with a gunshot to her head. It was ruled a suicide even though there were several packed suitcases as if she were going somewhere. Danny Ferguson was a co-defendant along with Bill Clinton in the Paula Jones lawsuit. Kathy Ferguson was a possible corroborating witness for Paula Jones.

13. **Bill Shelton** – Arkansas State Trooper and fiancée of Kathy Ferguson. Critical of the suicide ruling of his fiancée, he was found dead in June 1994 of a gunshot wound also ruled a suicide at the grave site of his fiancée.

14. **Gandy Baugh** – Attorney for Clinton's friend Dan Lassater, died by jumping out a window of a tall building in January 1994. His client was a convicted drug distributor. 14 – **Florence Martin** – Accountant & sub-contractor for the CIA, was related to the Barry Seal, Mena, Arkansas, airport drug smuggling case. He died of three gunshot wounds.

15. **Suzanne Coleman** – Reportedly had an affair with Clinton when he was Arkansas Attorney General. She died of a gunshot wound to the back of the head, which ruled a suicide. Was pregnant at the time of her death.

16. **Paula Grober** – Clinton's speech interpreter for the deaf from 1978 until her death on December 9, 1992. She died in a car accident.

17. **Danny Casolaro** – Investigative reporter investigating Mena Airport and Arkansas Development Finance Authority. He slit his wrists, apparently, in the middle of his investigation.

18. **Paul Wilcher** – Attorney investigating corruption at Mena Airport with Casolaro and the 1980 "October Surprise," was found dead on a toilet June 22, 1993, in his Washington DC apartment. He had delivered a report to Janet Reno 3 weeks before his death.

19. **Jon Parnell Walker** – Whitewater investigator for Resolution Trust Corp., Jumped to his death from his Arlington, Virginia, apartment balcony on August 15, 1993. He was investigating the Morgan Guaranty scandal.

20. **Barbara Wise** – Commerce Department staffer. Worked closely with Ron Brown and John Huang. Cause of death: Unknown. Died November 29, 1996. Her bruised, naked body was found locked in her office at the Department of Commerce. 21 – **Charles Meissner** – Assistant Secretary of Commerce, who gave John Huang special security clearance, died shortly thereafter in a small plane crash.

21. **Dr. Stanley Heard** – Chairman of the National Chiropractic Health Care Advisory

22. Committee died with his attorney, Steve Dickson, in a small plane crash. Dr. Heard, in addition to serving on Clinton's advisory council, personally treated Clinton's mother, stepfather, and brother.

23. **Barry Seal** – Drug running TWA pilot out of Mena, Arkansas, death was no accident?

24. **Johnny Lawhorn, Jr.** – Mechanic, found a check made out to Bill Clinton in the trunk of a car left at his repair shop. He was found dead after his car had hit a utility pole.

25. **Stanley Huggins** – Investigated Madison Guaranty. His death was a purported suicide, and his report was never released.

26. **Hershell Friday** – Attorney and Clinton fundraiser died March 1, 1994, when his plane exploded.

27. **Kevin Ives & Don Henry** – Known as "The boys on the track" case. Reports say the boys may have stumbled upon the Mena Arkansas airport drug operation. A controversial case, the initial report of death said, due to falling asleep on railroad tracks. Later reports claim the two boys had been slain before being placed on the tracks.

Many linked to the case died before their testimony could come before a Grand Jury.

The Following Persons Had Information On The Ives/Henry Case:

28. **Keith Coney** – Died when his motorcycle slammed into the back of a truck on 7/88.

29. **Keith McMaskle** – Died, stabbed 113 times, Nov. 1988

30. **Gregory Collins** – Died from a gunshot wound in January 1989.

31. **Jeff Rhodes** – He was shot, mutilated, and found burned in a trash dump in April 1989.

32. **James Milan** – Found decapitated. However, the Coroner ruled his death was due to "natural causes."

33. **Richard Winters** – A suspect in the Ives/Henry deaths. He was killed in a set-up robbery in July 1989.

The Following Clinton Bodyguards Are Also Dead

34. Major William S. Barkley, Jr.

35. Captain Scott J . Reynolds

36. Sgt. Brian Hanley

37. Sgt. Tim Sabel

38. Major General William Robertson

39. Col. William Densberger

40. Col. Robert Kelly

41. Spec. Gary Rhodes

42. Steve Willis

43. Robert Williams

44. Conway LeBleu

45. Todd McKeehan

It was also rumored that Bill Clinton flew to Jeffrey Epstein's island, called "Lolita Island."

Also, underage children accompanied Jeffrey Epstein and Bill Clinton to this island.

Bill Bowenhttps://youtu.be/fV_2HOAOGvo Innocence **Destroyed.**

So, is your memory of history challenged?

IS CPS the agency you THOUGHT it was?

IS ICE working to keep you safe?

What about the militarization of the Border?

IS President Trump responsible for the separation of families? What about CPS separating children from families IN THE UNITED STATES?

WHAT ABOUT TEXAS STATE SENATOR BOB HALL AND HIS CURRENT FIGHT WITH THE TEXAS CPS? What? You didn't hear about this? Read what the Texas Senator said on July 10, 2019:

Senator Bob Hall

July 10

Texas Child Protective Services (CPS) is spiraling out of control.

An agency that is supposed to be protecting our children may be the most dangerous to the well-being of young children. Even though the Texas Legislature appropriated the funding of $3.8 billion in All Funds, including $2.2 billion in General Revenue Funds, for all CPS functions at the Department of Family and Protective Services (DFPS), CPS still does not seem to know when it is necessary to take a child from its parents. In November 2018, a Houston Judge ordered a $127,000 sanction against CPS for the wrongful removal of children from their parents.

In the first week of July 2019, CPS successfully removed a four-year-old boy in

Kaufman County from his parents through the coordinated efforts of CPS, the Ad Litem attorney, a hospital doctor, and two courts. CPS forced this removal through the system without any evidence or firsthand testimony of any wrongdoing by the parents. Even the doctor, who first contacted CPS with a simple "concern" based solely on a partial review of medical records, told CPS, after meeting with the parents, that she saw no reason to remove the child from his parents. In typical CPS heavy-handed overreach, they ignored the doctor and preceded to cram the case through the court as an "emergency".

These are not isolated incidents. Now a federal appeal court has told CPS that it must fix its overburdened case load. However, there are many of us who recognize that it is much more than just case load that needs fixing at CPS.

I attended the hearing and have reviewed the 37-page document used by CPS. I will publish a four-part article describing what took place in the courtroom and what is in the official court documents.

So, this is the SECOND State Senator to address CPS for the corrupt agency it is.

You have read how Christopher Columbus kidnapped the INDIGENOUS people!

How rich white men kept kidnapping and trafficked humans from one country to another, then set their sites on the children, especially the poor and the children of immigrants.

How, in 1997, then President Bill Clinton, with the backing of his wife Hillary, signed the Adoption and Safe Families Act into law, allowing Child Protective Services to LEGALLY KIDNAP our children and give BONUSES to CPS social workers for each child removed?

How people like Nancy Schaefer and her husband, Bill Bowen, were found dead soon after investigating CPS corruption?

After reading this book, is there any doubt CPS cares less about the children and MORE about the money they make off of children?

How even former CPS investigators, like Carlos Morales, are saying they are trained to look at children as "walking bags of cash."

How people, like attorney Connie Reguli of Brentwood, Tennessee, are being targeted for helping families fight against CPS.

How children of immigrant families crossing the border are being separated, and that CPS is "cashing in" on this.

What will you do now?

Will you ignore what is going on? If you ignore it, MAYBE it will go away.

Will you fight against this agency that trains its people to look at children as "Walking bags of cash," and not as human beings who just want to be with family.

This problem won't go away because you ignore it and "hope it will go away!" Take action!

Contact the White House Comments: 202-456-1111

Switchboard: 202-456-1414

The White House

1600 Pennsylvania Avenue NW

Washington, DC 20500

Contact your representatives.

Protest! Do something to change what is going on.

Nothing will change unless YOU MAKE IT CHANGE!

Undeniable Fact: The jury has the power and jurisdiction to decide what is true and what is false, what is fact and what is fraud. This includes the ability to declare if a proposition that something is law, whether that is true or false, fact or fraud, law or not law, guilt or innocence. Law is a fact; fact is law, equity is law, and law is equity. Common law is the constitution, and the constitution is common law.

www.ingramcontent.com/pod-product-compliance
Lightning Source LLC
Chambersburg PA
CBHW072016150726
47999CB00002B/688